Collins

Treasure House

Pupil Book 4

Composition Skills

Author: Chris Whitney

William Collins' dream of knowledge for all began with the publication of his first book in 1819.

A self-educated mill worker, he not only enriched millions of lives, but also founded a flourishing publishing house. Today, staying true to this spirit, Collins books are packed with inspiration, innovation and practical expertise. They place you at the centre of a world of possibility and give you exactly what you need to explore it.

Collins. Freedom to teach.

Published by Collins
An imprint of HarperCollinsPublishers
The News Building
1 London Bridge Street
London
SE1 9GF

Browse the complete Collins catalogue at
www.collins.co.uk

ISBN 978-0-00-823649-6

British Library Cataloguing in Publication Data

A Catalogue record for this publication is available from the British Library

Publishing Director: Lee Newman
Publishing Manager: Helen Doran
Senior Editor: Hannah Dove
Project Manager: Emily Hooton
Author: Chris Whitney
Development Editor: Robert Anderson
Copy-editor: Trish Chapman
Proofreader: Tracy Thomas
Cover design and artwork: Amparo Barrera and Ken Vail Graphic Design
Internal design concept: Amparo Barrera
Typesetter: Ken Vail Graphic Design
Illustrations: Leesh Li (Beehive Illustration), Dante Ginevra, Adrian Bijloo, Aptara and QBS
Production Controller: Rachel Weaver
Printed and bound by Martins the Printers

Acknowledgements

The publishers wish to thank the following for permission to reproduce content. Every effort has been made to trace copyright holders and to obtain their permission for the use of copyright materials. The publishers will gladly receive any information enabling them to rectify any error or omission at the first opportunity.

HarperCollins Publishers Ltd for an extract on pages 4–5 from *The Hobbit* by J R R Tolkien, 1991, pp.13–14, copyright © The Tolkien Estate Limited, 1937, 1951, 1966, 1978, 1995. Reproduced by permission of HarperCollins Publishers Ltd; Peters Fraser & Dunlop for an extract on pages 7–9 from *The Stove Haunting* by Bel Mooney. Reproduced by permission of Peters Fraser & Dunlop (www.petersfraserdunlop.com) on behalf of Bel Mooney; Curtis Brown Group Ltd for an extract on page 11 from *Alice's Adventures in Wonderland*, dramatised by Clemence Dane, copyright © Clemence Dane, 1948. Reproduced with permission of Curtis Brown Group Ltd, London on behalf of The Beneficiaries of the Estate of Clemence Dane; Celia Warren for the poem on page 30 "Penguins on Ice" by Celia Warren, from *Wacky Wild Animals*, ed. Brian Moses, Macmillan Childrens Books, 2000, copyright © Celia Warren. Reproduced by kind permission of the author; Scholastic Inc. for the poem on page 31 "In Praise of Penguins" from *Learn All About Penguins* by Robin Bernard, Scholastic Inc./Teaching Resources, copyright © 1994 by Robin Bernard. Reproduced by permission; Judith Nicholls for the haiku on page 34 "Wolf", from *Midnight Forest* by Judith Nicholls, published by Faber & Faber, copyright © Judith Nicholls, 1987. Reproduced by kind permission of the author; and Dr Gervase Phinn for the haiku on page 35 "Seasonal haiku" by Richard Matthews from *Lizard over Ice*, edited by Gervase Phinn, published by Nelson Thornes Ltd, 1990, copyright © Richard Matthews; HarperCollins Publishers Ltd for the extract on page 63–64 from *Ruby-Rose* by Janet Foxley and Pedro Bascon, copyright © 2015 Janet Foxley; the extract on page 66–67 from *The Firebird* by June Crebbin, copyright © 2015 June Crebbin; the extract on page 69–70 from *The Four Desert Challenge* by Rob Alcraft, copyright © 2015 HarperCollins Publishers Limited; the extract on page 72 from 'What is Treasure?', published in *Treasure Box* by Pauline Stewart, copyright © 2013 Pauline Stewart; the extract on page 75–76 from Spider's Big Match' by Alan Durant, copyright © 2007 Alan Durant. Reproduced by permission of HarperCollins Publishers Ltd.

The publishers would like to thank the following for permission to reproduce photographs:

p.22 Digital Vision/Getty Images, p.23 Romolo Tavani/Shutterstock, p.24 MarcelClemens/Shutterstock, p.34 iStock/, Getty Images, p.35 (tl) worker/Shutterstock, p.35 (tr) iStock/, Getty Images, p.35 (br) Dennis van de Water/Shutterstock, p.35 (bl) George_C/Shutterstock, p.38 Arsgera/Shutterstock, p.39 Peter Hodgetts/Alamy Stock Photo, p.50 Stocktrek Images, Inc./Alamy Stock Photo, p.69 imageBROKER/Alamy Stock Photo, p.70 Alex Staroseltsev/Shutterstock.

MIX
Paper from
responsible sources
FSC C007454

FSC
www.fsc.org

Contents

Story settings

Read the extract from **'The Hobbit'** by **J.R.R. Tolkien**, then answer the questions that follow.

This is an extract from an adventure story. Bilbo Baggins is a hobbit on a journey with a group of dwarves, seeking treasure. In adventure stories, the characters often have to travel from a safe and comfortable setting into a setting that is grim and dangerous. This extract describes that change in setting.

It uses lots of adjectives for an atmospheric description.

Familiar setting

The characters are on a journey so the setting changes.

It sounds a lonely and unwelcoming place.

Personification ('evil' castles seem threatening)

The description tells us what the setting feels like as well as looks like.

At first, they passed through hobbit-lands, a wide respectable country inhabited by decent folk, with good roads, an inn or two, and now and then a dwarf or a farmer ambling by on business. Then they came to lands where people spoke strangely and sang songs Bilbo had never heard before. Now they had gone on far into the Lone-lands where there were no people left, no inns, and the roads grew steadily worse. Not far ahead were dreary hills, rising higher and higher, dark with trees. On some of them were old castles with an evil look, as if they had been built by wicked people. Everything seemed gloomy, for the weather that day had taken a nasty turn. Mostly it had been as good as May can be, even in merry tales, but now it was cold and wet. In the Lone-lands they had been obliged to camp when they could, but at least it had been dry ...

The weather and the darkness change with the setting, creating atmosphere.

Personification (trees that sigh seem sad and creepy)

Still the dwarves jogged on, never turning round or taking any notice of the hobbit. Somewhere behind the grey clouds the sun must have gone down, for it began to get dark as they went down into a deep valley with a river at the bottom. Wind got up, and willows along its banks bent and sighed. Fortunately the road went over an ancient stone bridge, for the river, swollen with the rains, came rushing down from the hills and mountains in the north.

Get started

Discuss these questions and complete these tasks with a partner.

1. Think of books you have read or that you are reading at the moment. Where are they set?

2. Which settings did you enjoy reading about? Why?

3. Which settings did you not enjoy reading about? Why?

4. Make a list of all the different settings you can think of.

Try these

The setting in the extract changes as Bilbo travels further away from his home. List the words and phrases that describe the hobbit-lands and those that describe the Lone-lands. Then write one or two sentences comparing the two settings. You could use the comparison conjunctions 'while' or 'whereas'.

Hobbit-lands	Lone-lands

Now try these

1. The weather changes on Bilbo's journey, making the atmosphere gloomier the further he travels. The same setting can feel very different depending on the weather. Make a list of what you might see and hear in these settings in good and bad weather. One has been done for you.

Setting	Good weather	Bad weather
A town centre	People in cafes, people wearing sunglasses, shadows on the ground	People with umbrellas, puddles, cars splashing water, miserable people
A rainforest		
Wide open fields		
A beach		

2. Read the extract again and look carefully at the techniques Tolkien uses to create atmosphere. Use your ideas for one of the settings from the previous activity to write two paragraphs creating two different pictures of the same setting.

Writing about a character

Read the extracts from **'The Stove Haunting'** by **Bel Mooney**, then answer the questions that follow.

When you create a character, just telling the reader about them isn't enough. You can also show the reader through what the character says and does, and how the other characters react.

Bel Mooney's story is set in the early 19th century. Farm workers were very poor. Some villagers in Winterstoke have been holding secret meetings to protest against low pay. One of these villagers is Thomas Leggat, but Daniel, a kitchen boy, discovers that Thomas is a spy.

> How characters react to each other tells the reader a lot about them.

There on the path stood Squire Plumtree himself, in his high polished boots and starched white neckcloth, talking to a man who wore the rough clothes of a labourer. Daniel recognised him at once – it was Thomas Leggat, one of the men whom Daniel had seen at the secret ceremony. Why would the Squire stand talking secretly in the cold darkness to a mere farm worker unless …? Daniel started to shiver.

The man glanced round nervously as he spoke, his eyes glinting in the light from the window like those of an animal at bay. The Squire had a peculiar look of pleasure on his face – not the kind that comes from happiness, but the kind which stems from black, grim satisfaction, as when an opponent has been defeated. Daniel strained his ears to hear. "… and so it is all arranged, and I suggest to you that you keep yourself indoors," the Squire was saying.

"Aye, master," mumbled Leggat.

"That will be all then … Oh, and here's payment for you. "

At that moment – he could not help it – Daniel sneezed.

Both men whirled round.

"Who's hiding there, in the name of God?" called the Squire in a furious voice.

Daniel stepped forward Into the light. "It's only me, your worship, with a letter from my master."

Daniel knows there is another secret meeting tonight and he wants to warn the others that Squire Plumtree knows about it.

Just as he reached the gates, however, a figure stepped out from the deeper blackness which encircled them, a figure that had been hiding in the thick bushes by the Manor entrance. It was a man – a tall man who reached

Adjective phrases are useful for describing characters.

What characters do and say shows the reader what they're like.

Adverbs give important information about how characters do and say things.

out a strong, bony hand which gripped Daniel painfully by the neck.

He wriggled but the grip tightened – viciously. And then a rough voice growled, "Now my young master, my little listener, I be wanting you to tell me where you're rushing off to, like." The tone was low and menacing, and as Daniel recognised it, his knees seemed to turn to water. It was Thomas Leggat – the man he now knew to be a spy.

Get started

Discuss these questions with a partner.

1. Which character or characters in the extract do you dislike?

2. Why do you feel the way you do about them? Look for evidence in the text.

3. Do you feel the same way about Daniel? Why?

Try these

Find the descriptions in the extract that tell the reader about Squire Plumtree and Thomas Leggat. The descriptions may be telling the reader something about their appearance or about their actions. Decide which and write them under the correct heading.

Name	Their appearance	Their actions
The Squire		
Leggat		

Now try these

1. Write a description of each character in this extract. Try to describe their personalities and what their actions tell us about them, as well as what they look like.

   a) The Squire

   b) Leggat

   c) Daniel

2. Read the last two paragraphs again where Daniel is on his way to the secret meeting to warn others. Rewrite this event from the point of view of Daniel (first person) and in the past tense. Include details about what Daniel thought and felt as Thomas Leggat held him, as well as describing what he did.

Writing a playscript

Read the playscript adapted from **'Alice's Adventures in Wonderland'** and dramatised by **Clemence Dane**, then answer the questions that follow.

Here is a playscript from a famous story. A playscript is the written instructions for a play (which is a performance of a story). A playscript should have everything the performers need to know to perform the story (what each character says and does, and descriptions of the settings). Because playscripts tell the performers what to say and do, everything is written in the third person and the present tense.

Alice has fallen down a rabbit hole into a very strange sort of place. She has met some very odd characters and, at this point in the play, seems to be lost.

A new scene starts whenever the play changes time or place. This scene is the fith scene in the play and takes place in a wood.

Spoken words are called 'dialogue'.

Scene 5: In a wood

Cheshire Cat: Miaw!

(Alice looks up. The Cheshire Cat is on a branch above her.)

Alice: Cheshire Puss!

(The Cheshire Cat grins. Alice crosses to the left of the Cheshire Cat.)

Would you tell me please which way I ought to go from here?

Cheshire Cat: That depends on where you want to go.

Alice: I don't care where …

Cheshire Cat: Then it doesn't matter which way you go.

Alice: What sort of people live about here?

Cheshire Cat: In one direction lives a Hatter, and in the other direction a March Hare. Visit either you like: they're both mad.

Alice: But I don't want to go among mad people.

Cheshire Cat: Oh, we're all mad here. You're mad. I'm mad.

Alice: How do you know that you're mad?

Cheshire Cat: To begin with, a dog's not mad. You grant that?

Alice: I suppose so.

Cheshire Cat: Well then, you see, a dog growls when it's angry and wags its tail when it's pleased. Now I growl when I'm pleased and wag my tail when I'm angry.

Alice: I call it purring, not growling.

Cheshire Cat: Call it what you like! Do you play croquet with the Queen today?

Alice: I haven't been invited yet.

Cheshire Cat: You'll see me there.

(The Cat vanishes.)

Get started

Discuss these questions with a partner.

1. Have you ever been to the theatre?

2. Has a theatre company ever come to your school to perform a play?

3. Have you ever read a play or acted in one?

4. Look at the playscript. How is the playscript different from a storybook?

Try these

Answer these questions and complete these tasks.

1. What do the names followed by colons tell the reader?

2. What is the technical name for the spoken words in a play?

3. What are stage directions for?

4. Why are stage directions in brackets?

5. In your own words, write a definition of a playscript.

6. Write a set of rules to follow for writing a playscript.

Now try these

1. Remember a conversation you've had recently or make one up. Answer these questions about the conversation.

   a) What was it about?

   b) Who was it with?

   c) Where did it happen?

   d) When did it happen?

   e) Exactly what was said (as best you can remember)?

   f) What did you and the other person (or people) do?

2. Write the conversation from question 1 as a full playscript. Include stage directions describing people's actions. Use this checklist to make sure you are writing the playscript correctly.

   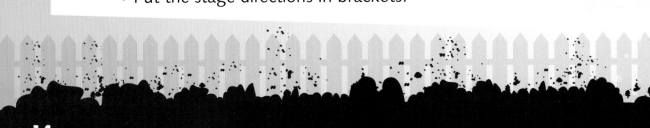

   - Write the details of where the scene is set at the beginning.

   - Don't use speech marks to show who is speaking.

   - Write the speaker's name followed by a colon to show who speaks each line.

   - Start a new line each time a character starts to speak.

   - Write stage directions to tell the performers what to do.

   - Write the stage directions in the third person and the present tense.

   - Put the stage directions in brackets.

Writing a realistic story

Read the extract from **'Secret Friends'** by **Elizabeth Laird** then answer the questions that follow.

A realistic story is a piece of fiction set in the real world. The story is made up but it has believable characters and dialogue, a real-world setting, and events that are possible in real life. It hasn't actually happened, but it could have happened. Realistic stories also deal with problems and issues that affect real people (like this story, which is about bullying and friendship).

> This is likely vocabulary for the narrator to use and it suits the setting.

> This story has a familiar, realistic setting.

It's crazy, starting a new school. For days you feel so new and lost it's as if you've wandered into a foreign country where you can't speak the language. Then, all of a sudden, everything falls into place and you feel you've been there forever.

The people fall into place too. It doesn't take long to work out who's going to be popular and who's going to be out of it, who's going to get into trouble and who's going to be teacher's pet.

It was obvious, from that very first day, that Rafaella was going to be an outsider, on the edge of everything, not liked. No one actually hurt or even teased her much. They just ignored her and left her out of things.

The dialogue sounds natural and informal.	"What do you want, Earwig?" a group of girls would say, as Rafaella approached them.
Scenes like this could be happening all the time.	They would stop their conversation to turn and look at her coldly, and she would blush, as she always did, mumble "Nothing," and turn away.
There aren't usually obvious heroes or villains in realistic stories.	I was in those groups sometimes, trying to talk to Kate and Sophie, the two super-popular girls in the class. And I'd watch Rafaella and think, not like that, you idiot. Smile. Say something cool. Don't show you care.

Get started

Discuss these questions and complete these tasks with a partner.

1. What do you know about the school and its children after you have read this extract? Discuss them with a partner and then write three facts.

2. Does the setting feel familiar? Do the characters feel familiar? Talk about things you recognise and relate to in the extract.

Try these

Answer these questions and complete these tasks.

1. What is the definition of a realistic story?
2. Where is this story set?
3. Is the setting a realistic setting? Why?
4. Who are the main characters?
5. Are the main characters believable? Why?
6. What themes are introduced in the extract?
7. Are these themes suitable for a realistic story? Why?
8. Find examples of realistic language and write them down.

Now try these

1. Have you, or someone you know, ever lost anything? Losing something is a popular theme for a realistic story. Plan your own realistic story by copying and filling in the story plan.

The thing, person or animal that is lost:		
Story title:		
Setting:		
Characters:		
Themes and issues:		
Beginning:	Middle:	End:

2. Read the extract again and look carefully at the annotations that explain the features of a realistic story. Write a scene from your realistic story based on the ideas in your story plan. Include some realistic dialogue between some of the characters you've planned.

Writing a good ending

Read the three possible story endings then answer the questions that follow.

At the end of a story, the problems characters have faced are resolved (for better or worse) and then any loose ends are tied up. If you haven't planned this stage, you might find yourself inventing messy or silly solutions just to make things tie up.

The story so far: Paul, Mandy and Ali are the last to leave the classroom at playtime. When everyone comes back in, Kate's lunchbox is missing. The teacher questions the three children and, although Paul has taken the lunchbox, all three of them say they know nothing about it. They are sent to the Headteacher.

This is an unhappy ending.

Ali has been blamed incorrectly. Wrong has been followed by more wrong.

Paul gets away with what he's done, which is frustrating.

A good ending doesn't have to be happy. Sad endings can be great to read about too. But, if they're really good, they might make you cry.

Ending 1

"Well," said the Headteacher. "What can you tell me about Kate's lunchbox?"

"Nothing," said Mandy. "I don't know anything."

"And you, Paul? What do you know about it?"

"I saw Ali take it," said Paul.

"That's not true," shouted Ali. "I left the classroom before you did."

"Well, Ali," said the Headteacher, "If Paul says you took it then that must be right. I shall have to ring your mother."

This is a happy ending.

Paul owns up, so wrong is put right.

The Headteacher is fair and understanding. Justice is done.

This is an unhappy ending.

The Headteacher is unfair and uncaring. Justice is not done.

Ending 2

"Well," said the Headteacher. "What can you tell me about Kate's lunchbox?"

"Nothing," said Mandy. "I don't know anything."

"And you, Paul? What do you know about it?" Paul just stood there, looking at the ground.

"I think Paul took it," said Mandy.

"So do I," said Ali. "He was the last in the classroom."

"Well, Paul? What do you say?"

"It was only a joke. I would have given it back."

"Well, Paul, you must return the lunchbox and you must apologise to Kate. We'll say no more about it this time, but if you are ever involved in anything like this again I will have to tell your parents."

Ending 3

"Come in, all of you," said the Headteacher in a stern voice. "Now I understand that you've all been involved in taking someone's lunchbox."

"No, I wasn't involved," protested Mandy.

"Nor was I," said Ali. "The teacher asked us about it because we were the last in the classroom before playtime."

"I really don't care," said the Headteacher. "As far as I'm concerned you're all to blame and you'll all be punished!"

Get started

Discuss these questions and complete these tasks with your partner.

1. Which ending did you like the best? Why?

2. Which ending did you like the least? Why?

3. Think of stories you have read and describe how they ended.

4. In the endings you've discussed, were all the problems resolved and were the loose ends tied up?

Try these

Answer these questions and complete these tasks.

1. What usually happens at the end of a story?

2. Why is it important to plan the ending of your story?

3. Does a good story ending always have to be a happy one?

4. Think of a story ending you liked. Write a review about why you liked it. What worked well? How did it make you feel?

5. Think of a story ending you didn't like. Write a review about why you didn't like it. What was bad about it? How did it leave you feeling?

6. Think of one fairy tale and write out the ending.

Now try these

1. Write a different ending for the story in the extract. Start with these lines from the extract. Plan some ideas and then write your ending.

   > The story so far: Paul, Mandy and Ali are the last to leave the classroom at playtime. When everyone comes back in, Kate's lunchbox is missing.

   - What happens next?

   - How is the problem resolved?

   - Is the lunchbox found? If so, where?

   - Will you give it a sad or a happy ending?

2. Read these problems faced by characters in stories. Choose one of the story plots and write a suitable ending for it.

   - Two friends are stranded on the rocks at the seaside and the tide is coming in.

   - Sam, a small boy, has wandered from his garden and is lost.

   - A family are going on holiday when their car breaks down.

More story settings

Look at this photo and the description that follows it, then answer the questions that follow.

There are lots of different techniques you can use to write really powerful descriptions. This short description of the Moonscape in the photograph shows you these techniques.

Preposition (to show where the things are that you describe)

Verb (shows what the things you describe are doing)

Adjective phrase (a group of words, some of which are adjectives, describing something)

Noun (an object or thing – the things you describe)

Adverb (describes the verb – how something is done)

Adjective (describing word)

Simile (a descriptive comparison using 'like' or 'as')

Metaphor (a descriptive comparison that leaves out 'like' or 'as')

Across the horizon the dusty, cratered surface of the Moon is silently still and lifeless. Overhead, like a jewel, hangs the brilliantly blue Earth, a fragile oasis of colour in the yawning black void of the sky.

Get started

Discuss these questions and complete these tasks with a partner.

1. Discuss what you know about the Moon and about space.

2. What do you think the surface of the Moon looks like?

3. What do you imagine it is like to be on the Moon?

4. List as many words as you can to describe the Moon. Use a thesaurus if possible.

Try these

The writer has used different techniques to describe the Moon. Copy the table and find the words and phrases in the extract and write them next to their technical name.

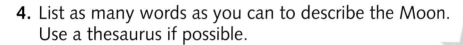

adjective	
preposition	
verb	
adverb	
simile	

Now try these

1. The writer describes the Earth as 'like a jewel'. This makes the Earth sound shiny and precious. This is called a simile: using one thing to describe another. Use a simile to describe each of these things. One has been done for you.

   a) He ran as _____ as a _____.

   Answer: *He ran as quickly as a cheetah.*

   b) The stars in the night sky _____ like _____.

   c) The water was as _____ as _____.

   d) The night sky was as _____ as _____.

   e) The ice _____ like _____.

   f) The car drove along the street as _____ as _____.

2. A new planet has been discovered. You have been sent to record what you see. In a short paragraph, describe the sight that greets your eyes as you step out of your space vehicle. Using the present tense, use noun phrases and prepositional phrases to describe what you see. Use a simile to make your descriptions more vivid for the reader.

Editing

Read these texts then answer the questions that follow.

Writers have to correct their work to improve it. This shows you some of the things you can do. Look at the corrections that have been made, and then read the edited version.

Don't say the same thing twice.	The astronaut looked around him ~~and looked~~ at the strange world. ~~It was very strange.~~ There was no movement and not a sound could be heard.
Use pronouns instead of repeating nouns.	~~The astronaut~~ᴴᵉ was standing on green rock which glowed. ~~The green rock~~ᴵᵗ stretched as far as he could see.
Add adverbs to show how things are done. Use conjunctions to join sentences. Use precise verbs.	He took a few steps forward. ~~He was cautious~~ᶜᵃᵘᵗⁱᵒᵘˢˡʸ because he did not know what to expect. The ground seemed firm,~~.~~ ~~When he took~~ᵇᵘᵗ ʷⁱᵗʰ his next step he sank into green sand. ~~He sank~~ᴵᵗ ᶜᵃᵐᵉ over his boots and ~~it was hard~~ʰᵉ ˢᵗʳᵘᵍᵍˡᵉᵈ to lift his feet up.

Edited version

The astronaut looked around him at the strange world. There was no movement and not a sound could be heard.

He was standing on green rock which glowed. It stretched as far as he could see.

He took a few steps forward cautiously because he did not know what to expect. The ground seemed firm, but with his next step he sank into green sand. It came over his boots and he struggled to lift his feet up.

Get started

Look back through your work this year. Discuss these questions and complete these tasks with a partner.

1. Can you find any work where you had to make corrections?

2. What corrections did you make and why?

3. Can you find any errors that still need correcting?

4. Make a note of any errors and corrections you find.

5. Are there any spelling, punctuation or grammar rules you need to revise?

Try these

The writer makes several errors in their writing about the astronaut. What can you learn from their errors? Make a list of these things as a reminder.

Now try these

1. The extract finishes with the astronaut in danger. Write the next part of the story from where the extract finishes:

   > The ground seemed firm, but with his next step he sank into green sand. It came over his boots and he struggled to lift his feet up.

2. Reread your work and check it for errors using the list you made previously. Check your spelling, punctuation, grammar and vocabulary. Could any of these be improved? If so, make the changes. Use a thesaurus if you need to. When you have edited your work and you are completely happy with it, read it aloud to a partner. Show them your work and ask for feedback. Then do the same for them. Remember to only give constructive criticism.

Writing settings

A. Write a few sentences as a description for each of the following settings:

- A snowy day
- A crowded street
- A busy classroom

A snowy day

A crowded street

A busy classroom

Character descriptions

B. Write a character description of a character from a book of your choice.

My character's name

Character description

Illustration of my character

Editing

C. Edit the writing below and check for spelling errors, punctuation errors and any opportunities for improving the vocabulary.

It wos a wet cald day and kamil was bored? he wonted to play fotbal wiv his freinds but the pich was waterlogged wat culd he do he cheked with his mum put on his rayncowt and ran to marks howse mark had the fotball game reddy on the computer kamil was pleesed he culd play fotbal with his freind adn not get wet at all

Different ways to write a poem

Read the poems below then answer the questions that follow.

These poems show you how two different poets write about the same topic in their own way.

Penguins on Ice

Three stanzas, each with six lines.

Every penguin's mum
Can toboggan on her tum.
She can only do that
As she's fluffy and fat:
 It must be nice
 to live on ice.

The rhyme scheme is AABBCC (the first and second lines rhyme, and the third and fourth lines rhyme).

Every penguin's dad
Is happy and glad.
He can slip and slide
And swim and glide:
 It must be nice
 to live on ice.

Each line has four or five syllables.

Each line has four or five syllables.

All penguin chicks
Do slippery tricks.
They waddle and fall
But don't mind at all:
 It must be nice
 to live on ice.

This is called a refrain (a repeated part of a poem).

Celia Warren

In Praise of Penguins

There are four stanzas, with four lines each.

These funny birds in fancy clothes
may waddle in the snow,
but when they reach the icy sea
Just watch how fast they go!

Addresses the reader directly.

Their song sounds like a donkey's bray,
they cannot soar or fly,
yet penguins manage very well,
and let me tell you why …

Most lines are alternately eight and six syllables long, which creates a 'waddling' rhythm.

Their feathers keep out water,
their blubber keeps out cold,
their wings make perfect paddles,
because they do not fold!

Their tails are good for steering,
they brake with both their feet –
So tell me now, from all you've heard …
Aren't penguins NEAT?

Robin Bernard

31

Get started

Discuss these questions and complete these tasks with a partner.

1. How does the second poem, 'In Praise of Penguins', describe penguins? Make a list of the words and phrases used to describe penguins.

2. How does the first poem, 'Penguins on Ice', describe penguins? Make a list of descriptive words and phrases from the poem.

3. What similarities and what differences can you find in the descriptions of penguins in the two poems?

Try these

These poems are structured very differently. Copy and complete the table with information about the two poems.

	Penguins on Ice	In Praise of Penguins
Number of stanzas		
Number of lines per stanza		
Number of syllables per line		
Rhyme scheme		
Refrain		

Now try these

1. Think of an animal that you want to write a poem about. Research some facts about your chosen animal. Think of poetic vocabulary you can use to describe it. Then copy and complete the table in order to plan and structure your poem.

This poem is about:
Animal facts and research:
Vocabulary to describe the animal:
Number of stanzas:
Number of lines per stanza:
Number of syllables per line (this can vary but should follow a pattern):
Rhyme scheme (if using one):
Refrain (if including one):

2. Now that you have planned your poem, write it out in full. Try to use some poetic devices, such as alliteration, personification, simile or metaphor if you can. Make sure you use plenty of descriptive, poetic language.

Writing haiku

Read these three poems then answer the questions that follow.

Haiku is a Japanese form of poetry and is one of the shortest poetic forms in the world. The point of a haiku is to capture and express a single idea (a moment, a feeling, an object, an animal or a person) in just three lines.

Haiku always follow the same structure. The first line has five syllables.

The last line should round off or sum up what the poem's all about.

Haiku don't normally rhyme.

Mark

Hair a tangled mop
Broken teeth and runny nose
That's my brother Mark.

Helen White

There are seven syllables in the second line.

There are five syllables in the third line; and 17 syllables altogether.

Wolf

still on his lone rock
stares at the uncaged star
cries into the night

Judith Nicholls

'Wolf' captures a single moment of a wolf howling in the night.

This poem is made up of four haiku, one for each season.

Haiku traditionally describe nature.

Seasonal Haiku

Buds full, fat and green
Pink blossoms trembling on trees
The warm breath of SPRING.

A burnished brass face
In an empty, cloudless sky
Smiles with SUMMER heat.

Curled and twisted leaves
Carpet red the cold dead earth.
AUTUMN'S withered hand.

Bitter winds of ice
Brittle grass like icy spikes
Old soldier WINTER.

Richard Matthews

Get started

Discuss these questions and complete these tasks with a partner.

1. Read and discuss each haiku.

2. Look carefully at 'Seasonal Haiku'. What do you notice about it?

3. Write a sentence for each haiku describing in your own words the picture it paints.

Try these

Use the example haiku and the annotations to answer these questions.

1. Where are haiku from?

2. What is the aim of a haiku?

3. How many lines do haiku have?

4. How many syllables are there in each line of a haiku?

5. Do haiku have a rhyme scheme?

6. What should the last line of a haiku do?

7. What are haiku traditionally about?

Now try these

1. Most haiku traditionally describe something in nature. If you were writing a haiku about the following things, what picture would you want to paint in the reader's mind? Write adjectives and/or noun phrases for each of these haiku topics. One has been done for you.

   a) A winter snowfall

   > Answer: *white snowflakes, thick carpet of snow, snowballs*

   b) A forest

   c) A thunderstorm

   d) The night sky

   e) A mountain

2. Choose one of the haiku topics and use your adjectives and noun phrases to write a haiku. Copy and complete the planning grid first, checking you have the correct number of syllables in each line, then write the haiku out in full.

Line	Syllables	Write the line here	
1	5		
2	7		
3	5		This should 'sum up' the rest of your haiku.

Making notes

Read the article about Mount Everest, then answer the questions that follow.

Selecting information and making notes are important skills that writers use all the time. This unit will improve your note-making skills, using this article about Mount Everest to practise on.

Mount Everest, at 8840 metres (29 002 feet or about 5.5 miles), is the highest mountain in the world. It is part of a range of very high mountains called the Himalaya to the north of India. These mountains are in Nepal and Tibet. They are so high that they are always covered in snow and ice. There is very little oxygen at these high altitudes, so climbers need to carry supplies of oxygen in tanks on their backs.

The mountain was named after Sir George Everest, who was the first to measure its height in 1849.

In the 1920s and 1930s, many teams of climbers attempted to reach the peak. All of these teams were helped by Sherpa people, who live in the mountains and know them well. They acted as porters, carrying food, tents and tanks of oxygen.

In 1952, a Sherpa called Tenzing Norgay worked with a Swiss expedition that climbed within 200 metres (656 feet) of the summit. This team had to turn back because of cold and exhaustion, but Tenzing learned a great deal from this experience. In 1953, he helped the British team succeed in reaching the summit. The team was led by John Hunt, but Tenzing Norgay and Edmund Hillary were the first at the top on 29 May 1953.

Teams still try to reach the summit today. Sadly, many are killed in the attempt. Some do succeed, though. In 1975, a group of Japanese women made the ascent and one of them, Junko Tabei, was the first woman to reach the summit.

Get started

Discuss these questions and complete these activities with a partner.

1. What is the main topic of this article?

2. Write a sentence describing the main topic in this article.

3. Look at the information in each paragraph and think of a subheading for each one.

Try these

Complete these tasks.

1. Find all the facts in the article about Sherpas and Tenzing Norgay. Write them in a bullet-point list.

2. Find all the facts in the article about women climbers. Write them in a bullet-point list.

3. Find all the facts in the article about the actual mountain, Mount Everest. Write them in a bullet-point list.

4. Use the information in the article to make a timeline from 1849 to 1975.

Now try these

1. Read the whole article again and consider the three headings in the table. Copy the table and add notes underneath the headings, taking the facts from the article.

Geography	Statistics	Climbers

2. Write a summary of the article describing what the article is about and what types of information is included in it. Try to use no more than 50 words.

Organising information (1)

Read the extract, then answer the questions that follow.

You can make information easy to understand by using headings, lists, bullet points and numbers. Paragraphs can be useful for particular topics or themes.

The main heading tells the reader what the whole text is about.	**SCHOOL SPORTS DAY** Our School Sports Day will be held at Nuffield Primary School on Thursday, 4th July. Each competitor will try to score points for their house. We will have three running races for each age group:

Bullet points are used to clearly separate items in a list.

- sprint

- skipping race

- egg and spoon race.

There will also be other events for KS2 children:

- high jump

- throwing the bean bag

- long jump

- obstacle race.

The afternoon will finish with running races for parents.

Timetables tell the reader when things are scheduled to happen.

Timetable

1:00   KS1 races
1:30   Y3 and Y4 jumping and throwing events
2:30   Y3 and Y4 races;
       Y5 and Y6 jumping and throwing events
3:00   Y5 and Y6 races
3:30   Mums' race
3:40   Dads' race

Prizes

There will be a badge and certificate for the first three in each race.

Numbered lists should be used when the order of things is important.

1. The winner of each race will score three points.

2. Second place will score two points.

3. Third place will get one point.

The house that gets most points at the end of the afternoon wins the athletics cup.

Reminders

Subheadings help you to organise your information and help the reader find specific information faster.

- Class 6 will be selling orange juice and biscuits, in aid of charity. Remember to bring your money!

- Each class will be exhibiting work they have done about their favourite sports in the hall.

- Bring your digital camera to get some great shots for the Best Sports Photograph competition!

Get started

Discuss these questions and complete these tasks with a partner.

1. How has the information in the extract been organised?

2. Make a list of the different organisational features and devices that have been used.

3. Why is it important to organise information?

Try these

Answer these questions about the extract.

1. How has information about the races been organised?

2. Which features tell the reader what each section is about?

3. How are the different event times organised and displayed?

4. Why are the prizes presented in a numbered list?

5. What information is presented in bullet-point lists?

6. What information has been presented in a short paragraph?

7. What does the main heading tell the reader?

Now try these

1. Imagine you are organising the end-of-term class party. Copy and complete the table, making notes under each heading.

Title of event	Date and time	Location	List of food to eat	Timetable of events

2. Using your party ideas, design a poster or flyer for your class party. Make sure it has all the information your classmates need to know and that it is organised clearly. Look back at how the information in the extract has been  organised and use some or all of the features from the extract: headings and subheadings, bullet-points or numbered lists, timetables and short paragraphs.

Writing notes for a newspaper report

Read these notes then answer the questions that follow.

When journalists report on events they make lots of notes.
Here are the notes a reporter made about a hospital fête.
The information in these notes can be organised into paragraphs
and written up in full sentences later.

Headings help to organise notes.

Newspaper articles report facts that answer the five questions: who, what, where, when and why?

Reporters interview people and quote them in their report.

'Hospital fête raises over £3500!' could be the headline. It should sum up the article and grab the reader's attention.

Event:

Caversham Hospital annual summer fête

Weather:

started hot and sunny, not a cloud in the sky until wind and thunderstorm came up suddenly

Attendance:

very well attended, hospital grounds full of adults (including nurses and doctors), children and lots of grandparents too!

Purpose:

to collect money for equipment for the children's ward; raised over £3500

Activities:

Army parachute display team – difficult jump because of windy conditions, although all but one parachutist landed on the target. The one who missed finished in the hospital car park with parachute caught on a lamp post.

Dashes can be used to save time when making notes.

Mini motorbike racing – nasty crash, but doctors and nurses quickly on scene and no serious injuries, though one child taken into the hospital!

Many other stalls and sideshows, including bouncy castle, always a favourite, welly throwing, tombola, wet-sponge throwing at the hospital administrator (seemed lots of the nurses were getting their own back).

As well as facts, the reporter might give opinions (known as speculation).

Get started

Discuss these questions with a partner.

1. What newspapers do you know of? What is your local paper? Does your school have a paper?

2. Have you ever read a report in a newspaper (paper or online)? If so, what was the story?

3. Have you (or anyone you know) ever been in a newspaper? If so, what was it for?

Try these

Read the reporter's notes about Caversham Hospital annual summer fête and answer the questions.

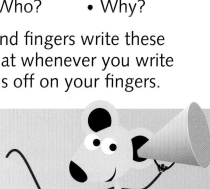

1. What was the event?

2. Who was there?

3. Why was it held?

4. What was the weather like?

5. Does the reporter write in full sentences? Why?

The bullet-point questions below – the '5Ws' – help news reporters to make good notes while they are at the events they write about. If they make notes about all five questions, they should have all the information they need to write a full report later.

- What?
- Where?
- When?
- Who?
- Why?

Draw around your hand. On your thumb and fingers write these five questions. Remember this picture so that whenever you write about an event you can count the questions off on your fingers.

Now try these

1. Think of an event that has happened at your school. It could be an author visit, a school trip, a school play, a class assembly or any other event that interests you. Copy and complete the table, thinking up a headline and writing notes to answer the questions about your event.

   These questions help news reporters to make good notes about the events they write about. Add a quote about the event from someone who was there. (If you can't get a real one, make one up.)

Headline:	
What?	
Where?	
When?	
Who?	
Why?	
Quote about the event:	
Person who gave the quote:	

2. Use the notes you made about your school event to write a report about it. Remember to write in full sentences. Add two or three sentences about something that went wrong at your event!

Writing an explanation

Read the report then answer the questions that follow.

This text is an explanation of how a famous disaster happened. The aim of an explanation text is always to answer a question of 'why?' or 'how?' This text answers the question 'How did the "Titanic" sink?'

How the 'Titanic' sank

Explanations are often full of facts and figures.

The passenger liner 'Titanic' was built in Belfast, Northern Ireland, in 1908–1912. She was 269 metres long and weighed 52 310 tons.

On 10 April 1912 she set off from Southampton on her maiden voyage. She carried 2224 passengers and crew. Some of the passengers were very rich, whilst others were fairly poor people going to America to start a new life.

When she was built, 'Titanic' was called 'unsinkable' as she had very modern safety features. However, she didn't have enough lifeboats for all the people on board. There were only enough for 1178 people so, when disaster struck, 1502 people died.

So how did this 'unsinkable' ship sink?

These simple drawings are diagrams.

Diagrams have to be simple to give information as clearly as possible.

These diagrams explain, stage by stage, why 'Titanic' sank.

These are captions. They add information and clarity to each diagram.

This photograph shows the reader what 'Titanic' really looked like.

Compartments

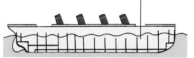

Air could flow from one compartment to another.

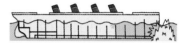

In the foggy waters near Newfoundland, 'Titanic' hit an iceberg that punctured five of her 16 compartments. It happened at 23:40 on 14 April.

Water filled the punctured compartments, but it also flowed into those that were not damaged.

By 2:10 on 15 April, the decks were under water. 'Titanic' broke in two and sank to the bottom of the sea.

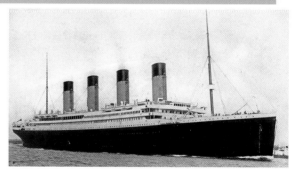

Get started

Answer these questions and complete these tasks with your partner.

1. Think of some 'how?' questions you would like the answers to. Make a list.

2. What questions do you already know the answers to? Make a list.

3. Each choose a question you know the answer to.

4. Provide each other with an explanation for your chosen question.

Try these

1. What is the aim of an explanation text?

2. What information do the four diagrams show?

3. What are captions and what is their purpose?

4. What does the photograph show the reader?

5. Write a short summary of the information included in each paragraph.

6. Copy out any technical language the writer has used. Look it up in a dictionary if you need to.

Now try these

1. Think of something you are learning about or that you are interested in. Ask a 'why?' or 'how?' question about it. What diagrams could you use to help explain the answer? What captions or labels would you need? Copy and complete the table in order to plan an explanation text of your own.

Question:	
Answer:	
Diagrams:	
Captions:	
Other features (such as headings, labels, lists):	
Technical language needed:	

2. Using the notes you have made, write your explanation text. Remember, the aim is to answer the question you have chosen, explaining things as clearly as possible to your reader. Share your finished text with your partner and check that they understand your explanation. Then do the same for them.

Writing an instruction text

Read these instructions, then answer the questions that follow.

A set of instructions is a non-fiction text that explains to the reader how to do something. Instructions must be clear and easy to follow. Here are some instructions to make a hovercraft.

Diagrams show the reader what to do in a way that words can't.

The main heading states the aim of the instructions.

Equipment is listed first so the reader can make sure they have it all before they start.

Making a hovercraft

You will need:

- scissors
- stiff paper
- ruler
- pencil or pen
- paints or colouring pens
- sticky tape
- balloon

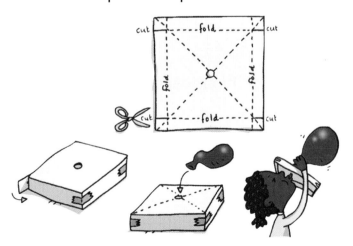

What to do:

1. Cut a piece of paper 12 cm × 12 cm.

2. Measure 2 cm from each of the four sides and draw lines.

3. Find the centre of the paper by drawing two diagonal lines. Where they meet is the centre.

4. In the centre, cut a hole about the size of a small coin.

5. Make four short cuts, one on each corner, as shown in the diagram.

6. Colour your hovercraft.

7. Fold in the corners as shown to make a box shape.

8. Use the sticky tape to hold the corners in position.

9. Pull the balloon through the hole and blow it up from underneath.

The finished model should look like this.

Other ideas:

Try making hovercrafts of other shapes and sizes.

Get started

Discuss these questions with a partner.

1. When have you had to follow a set of instructions? What were they for?

2. Have you ever written any instructions before? What were they for?

3. What is the most important thing about instructions?

Try these

Complete the tasks and answer the questions about the instructions for making a hovercraft.

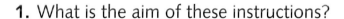

1. What is the aim of these instructions?

2. Why have diagrams been included?

3. Why are the instructions presented in a numbered list?

4. What are imperative verbs?

5. Find all the imperative verbs and make a list.

6. Find examples of positional language and write them down.

Now try these

1. Choose something that you know how to make and write a set of instructions for making it. Only use resources and equipment that are available. Copy and complete the table to help you organise your instructions and to make sure you do not leave anything out. Draw diagrams with the instructions to make things as clear as possible.

Title: Instructions for making a _____	
Equipment:	
Instructions (including diagrams):	
Any additional comments:	

2. Swap instructions with a partner. They follow your instructions and you follow theirs. Gather the resources and the equipment you need.

Then follow each step carefully to the end. Afterwards have completed the instructions, give feedback on how easy the instructions were to follow. Was there anything your partner forgot to include? Your partner should do the same for you.

Writing an explanation

A. Draw a simple flowchart to explain how a plant grows. Two of the illustrations have been done for you. Label each stage by writing a complete sentence beneath.

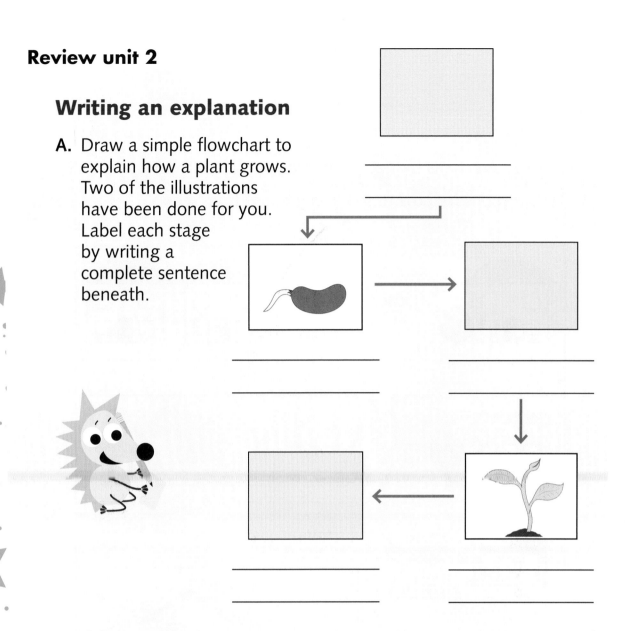

Writing a newspaper report

B. Imagine your school has just competed in the Schools Cup Final. Write a report of the match for your school newspaper.

The School Times

Writing an instruction text

C. Write directions for how to get to your house from the school.

Directions for how to get to my house from school.

Writing a letter

Read the letter of complaint, then answer the questions that follow.

When writing a formal letter, you should use formal language and Standard English throughout. How you sign off depends on whether you know the name of the person you're writing to or not. If you know, the name use 'Yours sincerely'; if you don't, use 'Yours faithfully'. Whether you know the person or not, you can always sign off with 'Yours truly'.

Jenny's address	
The date Jenny wrote the letter.	23 Centre Crescent Upper Blaxland Suffolk XI 2YY Wednesday 4 July 2015
Greeting	Dear Mr Smith,
The structure of the letter is important.	Last week I bought a new bike from your shop. At first I was very pleased with it, but already things have started to go wrong.
Jenny explains why she is writing and what she is writing about.	When I came into the shop to tell you about it, the assistant said that you are on holiday and that I should write a letter.

Jenny states what the main problem with the bike is.	The worst thing is that Mum and I cannot tighten the saddle, no matter how hard we try. This means that it moves slightly as I am riding along. I think you would agree that this is very dangerous.
A list of other little problems with the bike.	There are other problems as well. The bell is stiff and doesn't ring properly, the brakes on the back wheel are rubbing and the left-hand pedal squeaks.
An example of formal language.	As I had to save for a long time to buy my bike at a rather high price, I'm sure you will agree that these things should be put right. 
The aim is to persuade Mr Smith to put things right.	Yours sincerely, Jenny Lindman

Get started

Discuss these questions and complete the tasks with a partner.

1. Have you ever written a letter? Have you ever received a letter?

2. Why do people write letters? Think of as many reasons as you can and write them down.

3. Do you think that people mostly write emails now instead of letters? Do the same rules apply?

Try these

Answer the questions and complete the task.

1. What is the aim of Jenny's letter?

2. How does Jenny end her letter?

3. Does Jenny know Mr Smith personally?

4. What sort of language does Jenny use?

5. What has Jenny included in the top right of her letter?

6. Write a summary of each paragraph of Jenny's letter.

Now try these

1. Imagine you have been asked to write a letter of complaint to your local council about one of the following:

- Parking outside your school, which is endangering children

- Litter in the streets outside your school

- No play facilities for children in your local area.

Think about what your main argument is and what you would like the council to do about it. Plan your letter under these headings in the table.

Address and date	(Where will this go?)
Formal greeting	(Do you know their name?)
First paragraph	(What has happened to make you write this letter?)
Second paragraph	(What do you want the council to do?)
Signing off	(If you know the person's name, use 'Yours sincerely'; if you don't, use 'Yours faithfully'.)

2. Write your letter of complaint using the planning table to remind you of what to include. This time you should write in full sentences and use formal language.

Characters in narrative

Read the following extract from '**Ruby-Rose**' by **Janet Foxley and Pedro Bascon** and then answer the questions that follow. Ruby-Rose is on her way to Grandma's house. Her mother has warned her not to take the short cut through the forest as two children have recently gone missing.

The author uses this adverb – describing the way Ruby-Rose says something to her mother – to tell us something about her character.

"All right, all right," Ruby-Rose agreed impatiently. "I won't go through the forest."

Because it was a warm, sunny day, Ruby-Rose chose the red hat with the wide shady brim. Then she picked up the basket and kissed her mother goodbye.

Throughout the extract the author both shows the reader what the character is like through their actions and tells us directly. Here we are shown that Ruby-Rose is affectionate and loves her mother.

It was a *very* warm, sunny day and the basket was heavy. By the time she got to the beginning of the path through the forest, Ruby-Rose was already feeling tired.

She put her basket down for a few moments to rest her arms. *I really don't want to go all the way round by the road, she thought. It's so much further. Mother always worried too much. I know the forest paths very well. I'm not going to get lost.*

The author lets us know what Ruby-Rose is thinking. This gives us deeper insight into her character.

She picked up her basket and set off down the path through the forest, quite forgetting what her mother had said about the hunters finding the girl's and the boy's shoes.

Here the author tells us how Ruby-Rose is feeling in a direct way.

At first Ruby-Rose was happy that she'd come this way. It was cool under the trees. Sunlight filtered through the branches and birds were singing. But as she went further, things changed. The trees closed over her head, casting shadows so deep that she could hardly see where she was treading. The birds fell silent. Now all she could hear were her own footsteps. And other, softer footsteps.

Here it as if we are seeing things directly through Ruby-Rose's eyes. In this way we feel her growing fear.

Get started

Discuss these questions with a partner.

1. As you read the passage, does another traditional tale come to mind? What clues are given?

2. What do you think about the character Ruby-Rose? Do you like her? Would you act like her in a similar situation?

3. How does the author reveal her personality and mood to the reader?

Try these

Answer the questions from the story.

1. Write a sentence to describe Ruby's Rose's character at the beginning of the extract.

2. Now write another sentence to describe how our understanding of Ruby's Rose's character has changed and deepened by the end of the extract.

3. We learn about Ruby-Rose's character in different ways. Copy and complete the following table.

Examples where the author tells us directly	Examples where the author shows us her actions	Examples where the author shows us her words and thoughts

Now try these

1. Write a paragraph showing how Ruby-Rose's character and mood develop through the story. Write a sentence for each stage.

2. Continue the story as she walks deeper into the forest. Keep the tension and create atmosphere as she believes she is being followed. Use the different ways highlighted in the extract to let the reader know more about Ruby-Rose's character as she faces danger. Is she going to be brave, clever, fearful, stupid...?

Plots in folk tales

Read the following extract from '**The Firebird**' by **June Crebbin** and then answer the questions that follow.

'The Firebird' is a famous Russian folk tale. Folk tales are stories that have been passed on in spoken form, from one generation to the next. Usually, the author is unknown and there are many versions of the tale. Folk tales could be fables, fairy tales or old legends.

Long ago, in a far and distant land, there lived a king called Damon. He was so rich that in his garden grew a tree full of golden apples.

King Damon loved this tree and kept a strict count of all the apples. One day, he found that someone was visiting his garden at night and stealing a golden apple. Every morning, one more was missing.

The king sent a servant to watch for the thief, but the night was long and the servant, sitting down by a bush, soon fell asleep. In the morning another apple had disappeared.

"I didn't close my eyes," the servant told the king, "but I saw no one."

After three nights, when the thief had been neither seen nor heard, Ivan, the King's son, offered to keep watch himself.

As darkness fell, Ivan went into the garden. He made himself walk about near the tree, afraid to sit down in case he fell asleep. An hour went by, and another, and a third. Half the night had passed when Ivan noticed something glowing in the distance. The light came closer and closer until the whole garden was lit up as if by a thousand rays of sunshine.

Ivan kept very still. As he watched, he saw a firebird fly up into the tree of golden apples. Quietly, Ivan crept nearer, but just as he reached up to catch the thief, the Firebird, startled, flew away, leaving only a feather in Ivan's hand. As soon as his father was awake, Ivan showed

him the feather and told him who the thief had been.

From that time, although the Firebird didn't visit the garden again, the king couldn't stop worrying that it might.

Ivan, seeing his father so saddened, mounted his horse, Arkady, and rode away to seek the firebird. One day, Ivan reached a spot where the road branched off in three different directions. There stood a huge stone. On it was written:

"Go straight and you will never be seen again.

Go to the right and you will lose your horse.

Go to the left and you will die."

Get started

Discuss these questions with a partner.

1. Do you know any folk tales? Any folk tales from other countries? Tell one to your partner.

2. Why do you think there are many versions of some folk tales?

3. In your family, are there any tales or stories that have been passed down from earlier generations?

Try these

Answer the questions from the story.

1. In the first two sentences what feature of folk tales are we introduced to?

2. How does the king know that one apple is missing?

3. Why does the king's son, Ivan, decide to keep watch?

4. What proof does Ivan have of who the thief was?

5. Why does Ivan ride off to seek the bird?

6. Which of the three choices would you make if you were Ivan?

7. Do you know any other traditional tales, folk tales or stories where things happen in threes? This feature is often seen in these types of story.

Now try these

1. Create a story board to retell the events of the folk tale so far. Add the narrative to the pictures.

2. Using a branch diagram, plan what will happen in the plot if Ivan takes the different paths.

Organising information (2)

Read the following extract adapted from '**The Four Desert Challenge**' and the panels about some of the features of information texts. These help organise the information clearly and help the reader to make their way round the text.

This is the main heading.

Information texts provide lots of precise facts – how far, how long, how many, etc.

This is a subheading.

Extra facts and interesting information are often added in the form of boxes.

THE RACE IS ON

The Four Desert Challenge is one of the world's toughest running events. The challenge is four races, across four deserts. Competitors who run all four races must complete a total of 28 days' racing. They must run over 1000 kilometres in some of the wildest and loneliest places on Earth.

The participants

The four races are held every year, one after the other. Some runners in the Four Desert Challenge are Olympic athletes who compete to win. Athletes like these sometimes run all four races in a single year. Other competitors take longer, running only one race a year. Many compete in teams, helping and encouraging each other when the going gets hard – which it often does!

Each desert race is six stages, run one after the other over seven days.

Covering the distance

Most stages are 40 kilometres – about the same distance as a marathon. There's a set time to finish each stage, but it's long enough so that competitors don't have to run the whole way – walking is allowed!

Each race also has a stage called the Long March, which is over 80 kilometres. This is the toughest part of every race, and is included to really push racers to their limits.

There are checkpoints along the race route where the competitors can get water and medical help if they need it. In every race there is a team of doctors who volunteer to look after the competitors.

Runners wear head torches so they can see where they are going.

Each paragraph deals with a clear separate sub-topic.

Get started

Discuss these questions with a partner.

1. Have you ever been in a race of any kind? Discuss this and talk about what it was like to participate, to win or lose, to complete the race and to train for the race.

2. What do you think makes a person want to take part in the Four Desert Challenge?

3. Which famous athletes can you name? Which specific runners can you name? Are there any good runners in your class or in your school?

Try these

Answer the questions about the text.

1. How many types of heading are there in the extract? List the headings under each type.

2. Why do you think the headings are shown in different ways?

3. List all the number-related facts in the extract.

4. What verb tense is used to present the information?

5. List five examples of verbs used in this tense.

6. Where do you find the contents page in a book and what do you find there?

Now try these

1. The information below is an extract from the contents page of '**The Four Desert Challenge**'. Write two or three sentences about what you would expect to read in these different sections.

   Get set for the heat

   Ready, steady pack!

   Destination China

   Glossary

2. Find out about different types of running events at the Olympics. Write a short information text about them.

Writing list poems

Read the poem below and answer the following questions.

The poem's structure is provided by the repetition of 'It is...'

The poem takes the form of a series of very brief stanzas, at most two lines long.

The poem reaches an emotional conclusion or high point with this sentence.

What is Treasure?

It is the first cry of a new baby
(Life being the greatest treasure of all).

It is the smell of new grass.

It is many buffalo moving across
the plain as one shadow.

It is the much water after the dry season.

It is the feel of a cool
breeze on a hot day.

It is the smell of a
meal after hunger.

It is friends.

It is happiness.

Pauline Stewart

Get started

Discuss these questions with a partner.

1. Write a list of the things you have done today since you woke up. Share the list with your partner.

2. In what way is the poem a list? Why would the poet choose to write her poem in the form of a list?

3. Why does the poet consider all these things as 'treasure'?

Try these

Answer the questions from the poem.

1. What is the 'greatest treasure' of all according to the poet?

2. What are buffalo? Look this word up in a dictionary.

3. What is a plain? Look this word up in a dictionary.

4. Why does the author say that the buffalo are 'moving across the plain as a shadow'? What does it mean?

5. Why do you think the poet separates each line beginning 'It is...' into its own stanza?

Now try these

1. What is your treasure? What things are as precious to you as the things in the poem are to the poet? Make a list of your 'treasure' and write it in the same way as the poet has done.

2. Write a list poem using the structure provided in 'What is Treasure' ('It is...'). Call it 'What is a Friend?' Think of all the ideas you have about this and write them in the form of a list poem. Try to end the poem with a clear conclusion.

Writing recounts

Read the following extract from '**Spider's Big Match**' by **Alan Durant** and then answer the following questions.

Everyone says that Spider McDrew is a hopeless case. His mind wanders and he is always one step behind everyone else. After many of the players in the football team catch chickenpox, the class teacher calls on Spider to play. The first half of the match doesn't go well for Parkfield School; the second half has to be better...

Straight from the kick-off, Parkfield went on the attack. They passed the ball around carefully, waiting for an opening. Spider played his part, running hard and not giving the ball away once. Parkfield got a corner and another one … they had lots of shots. They hit the bar and the post. But still a goal would not come. Then, with ten minutes left, Jason Best burst through the Stoneley defence and, as the goalkeeper came out, he chipped the ball beautifully … just over the bar.

"Great try!" shouted the Parkfield crowd. The next time Spider got the ball, he kept it instead of passing. He turned past one defender …

nutmegged a second, pushing the ball between his legs …

and skipped over the tackle of a third.

The Parkfield crowd bayed with excitement as Spider swerved past the last defender and sent the Stanley goalkeeper tumbling into the mud. The goal was at Spider's mercy. No one could catch him.

"Shoot!" cried the crowd.

With great care, Spider drew back his foot and chipped the ball ... just over the bar, exactly as his captain had done.

For a moment there was a shocked silence. The players of both sides stood stock-still, boggle-eyed. The crowd lost its voice. Mr Smithers, who had been about to blow for a goal, nearly swallowed his whistle. Jason Best rushed up to Spider and pushed his finger into his chest.

"You useless idiot, Spider," he said. 'What were you thinking of?"

"I was trying to do what you did," Spider said unhappily. "I'm sorry."

"Sorry?" said his captain fiercely. "You've just lost us the championship."

Get started

Discuss these questions with a partner.

1. Have you ever played in a team match of any kind? Share what it felt like to either win or lose. If you haven't ever played in a match, what is it like when a team you like or support loses?

2. Where might you find a recount or report of a football match?

3. Do you think the author wants the reader to support Parkfield's football team? What evidence is there for or against your point of view?

Try these

Answer the questions from the story.

1. Why is this match so important for Parkfield?

2. In the second paragraph what does Spider do to excite the crowd?

3. What reason does Spider give for kicking the ball over the bar?

4. Why is it important to recount the events of the match in sequential or chronological order? This means in the order in which they happened.

5. Find adverbs in the extract. Why has the author used these?

6. What verb tense is used in this recount of the match?

7. Who is recounting the events – Spider? Mr Smithers? The Staneley goalkeeper? A narrator? Jason Best?

Now try these

1. Imagine you are Spider. You are going to plan a recount of the match. This is called a first-person recount because you (as Spider) are telling the reader what happened in the match. You will need to list, in sequence, the events of the second half of the match and add any information from the extract that you feel is important.

2. You are Spider. Write a recount of the second half of the football match in your diary. Make sure that, as well as writing what happened, you say how you felt at the time.

Planning a plot

A. Choose one of the titles below and plan a narrative plot of your choice. Use the planner provided.

- The Secret Door

- Stranded!

- I said to my friend, "I'm never going back there again!"

Title:	
Setting:	
Characters in my narrative:	
How my story will start:	
How my story will develop – what will happen next?	
Will my main character change? How?	
How my story will end:	

Writing an information text

B. Write a fact file (information text) about your hobby or pastime.

Introduction	
Information 1	
Information 2	
Information 3	

Writing a recount

C. Think of a special event that the school has held recently and write a third-person recount (using 'he'/'she'/'they' rather than 'I') about this event.

Title:
My recount

BURLESQUE

THE MOTION PICTURE

INTRODUCTION BY CHER / FOREWORD BY CHRISTINA AGUILERA

WELCOME TO BURLESQUE BY STEVEN ANTIN

UNIVERSE

*T*he first time I walked into Grauman's Chinese Theatre I knew something was about to happen that would change my little life forever. And, it was going to happen in this huge, radiant palace, just like the ones my mother told me stories about. My mother and father brought me to see my first film.

As I walked in, wearing my little patent leather Mary Janes, I knew I was home. I'm not kidding. The beautiful ushers and usherettes scurrying around in their Chinese costumes mesmerized me. One of them came up to my parents and asked for our tickets. She then took out a magic wand (I later learned it had another name–*flashlight*) and guided us to our seats. It was heaven with popcorn!

Then it happened: The lights went off, the curtain went up, and on came pure magic…it was called *Cinderella* and I knew, from the moment she opened her mouth to sing, that that was what I would do when I grew up! I was spellbound. I didn't even realize I was watching a cartoon—no humans anywhere. I didn't even notice that small detail! I walked out, no, that's not completely correct. I *floated* out of the theater and into the backseat of our car. And then, without saying a word to my parents, I proceeded to sing "A Dream Is a Wish Your Heart Makes" from memory! Out of the corner of my eye I saw my mother jab my father. She said, "John, listen. She's singing the song from the movie word for word and note for note." My mom was a singer and she knew, we both knew, right then and there that the only thing for me was to be *Cher*. Well, I've been *Cher* for forty-five years, but it's taken me sixty years to make my dream come true! I'm finally getting to sing and act in a film—just like Cinderella.

Burlesque is one of the toughest jobs I've ever loved. Most of the girls were half my age, beautiful, talented, and a blast to work with.

I watched Christina, an incredible singer and dancer with one of the most exceptional voices I've ever heard, change before my eyes into a fine actress. It was wonderful to see that happen. Of course, me being me, I had to give her one tiny bit of advice. It was in the scene in which Tess says, "OK, I'm going to build the show around you." There was a close-up on Christina, and though she had a beautiful look on her face, I knew she had more to give. I went up to her and said, "Christina, this is the moment you've been waiting for all your life. Not your character's life but *yours*. It's now or never. Moments later I watched her pull years of tears out of those baby blue eyes. Yeah! I know this beautiful child can go as far, and as deep, as she wants to go. I'm proud of her and I am proud to be in this film with her.

(CONTINUED)

Working with Stanley was one of the joys of my life. Meryl and I talked about him and we both agree, he's one of the best actors we've ever worked with. He never has a false moment in any of his performances. Frankly, it pisses me off.

K-Bell is a firecracker of a girl! We went toe-to-toe in our fight scene, and after it was over, we both needed pedicures!

Peter is a wonderful, fun, and easy actor. You can just grab him by the hand and say, "OK Peter, lets jump," and he'll say, "OK with me Cher, we're jumping in!"

I've known Eric since he was a teenager, and he has charisma oozing out of his pores.

Cam has a kind of James Dean quality; I can't really explain how or why. It's just a look he sometimes gets in his eyes.

I was really touched as I watched tears drip over Julianne's lashes during our one tender scene together. I said, "Babe, save some for your close-up, we want *everyone* to see them!"

Steven Antin, our director, exhibited the characteristics I've seen in the best directors I've worked with. He was calm, loving, and open to ideas. Steven let me write a scene between Christina and me two days before we shot it! It was a little scene about a real-life experience I had had as a kid, watching my mother and her friends putting on their makeup together through our big back window. They were all so beautiful, and I was an ugly duckling. I couldn't wait to grow up and paint my face like they did!

I must mention Clint Culpepper, the head of Screen Gems, next. Words cannot do Clint justice. He is almost always the funniest, most clever, and smartest man in the room, and he is always working! I believe he sleeps standing up at the studio. He grabbed my hand and threw me into this film, telling me he wouldn't let go until I was finished. Clint was true to his word, and I'm almost positive I'll get my hand back by the end of the year.

Amy Pascal, the chairman of Sony Pictures, has to be thanked next. She made me feel that I was the one woman who could play Tess. I'm always surprised when someone says anything like that to me, but it gave me the confidence to take risks. A great director once told me "If you're not willing to look ridiculous you can never be great!" I can't thank Amy enough and hope her faith in me will be justified.

Risa Shapiro has been my friend and agent forever, despite the fact that I've pretty much been on the road the entire time. Anyone else in this town would have gotten frustrated and blown me off years ago, but not my Risa! She's with me till the bitter end! God love her.

I want to thank my managers, Roger Davies and Lindsay Scott, who have always been there for me. They are always there for all their girls, including Tina, Pink, and Sade. At least they have me, their one hassle-free client. NOT! Yet they love me, and the feeling is mutual.

There is one person to whom I owe a deep debt of gratitude, who, for some unknown reason (beside the fact that we've adored each other for over thirty-five years) told Clint, "Cher is the *only* actress who can play the part of Tess," then e-mailed me and wrote "Sweetheart, I've just read a great script and you've got to do it!" Now everyone who knows me knows how stubborn I am, but when my friend David says, "Sweetheart, you've got to do something," I listen! David Geffen is the smartest person I know, and I will never be able to thank him enough for helping to give me one of the most fulfilling experiences I've ever had.

I could fill this book with the names of all of the special people that I want to thank, but since we have a limited amount of space, I'll write their names and put the first words that come into my mind.

Bojan Bazelli: A true genius DP. I will *never* look this good again.

Donald De Line: Sent me one of the greatest ego-boosting text messages I've ever received.

Leonard Engleman: My friend, and the man who puts the "artist" in "makeup artist." We've been together for more than twenty-four years, and even after all that time, he'll still stand back after working for over an hour on my face and say, "Just a little touch of color to add to the beauty that's already there."

Serena Radaelli: A genius with hair, and the epitome of the Italian woman: sexy, rowdy, and unable to talk without her hands!

Rosemarie Capalutti: We've been together for twenty-four years and she takes care of my costumes, and me, like we were her children! Another fab thing about Rosie is she's always laughing, which makes her worth her weight in sparkly things!

Morgan Bernhard: A wiz with wigs. The dry wit that comes from between those little French-speaking lips fits perfectly within the rest of this giggly, high-spirited, ass-kicking woman!

Carol Robinson: Made all the wigs for this film, so you can see she's the best! Plus, she loves to laugh. Do you see a pattern here?

Deb Paul: My unbelievable assistant for thirty-one years. This wonderful woman was there for me through *Witches, Suspect,* and *Moonstruck.* Even though she wasn't able to be on set with me as much as we wanted this time because she was too busy working her tail off taking care of all the craziness at my house, her presence was always felt.

Warren Grant: My friend and business manager who is always behind the scenes looking out for me.

Last, but certainly not least, is Jennifer Ruiz: She shook me awake in the dark and pointed me toward my bed in the morning light. Jen was always trying to help make my life on the set as easy as possible during the many sixteen hour days. And without complaining! Jen's a very "Don't cry, you're fine" kind of girl! She's a true Taurean, she'll laugh when she wants to cry and she's the one girl you want in your foxhole.

Burlesque was one of the most wonderful, tough, artistically fulfilling experiences I've ever laughed and cried my way through.

And don't tell Clint, but I would have done it for free.

—CHER

*T*he world of burlesque has always intrigued me. The mind-blowing performers, their titillating movements, the lavish costumes, provocative music, dramatic lighting, and satire have always managed to raise eyebrows, generate laughs, and get hearts thumping. In many ways, burlesque style has had an influence on my music over the years, but it wasn't until I received a unique script from renowned studio chair Amy Pascal and studio chief Clint Culpepper that I truly began to understand and appreciate the essence of the world itself.

The studio and its producer, Donald De Line, gave me the opportunity to live and breathe burlesque, and I was determined to put my heart and soul into the craft. I'll never forget the day I was introduced to director Steven Antin. I felt I'd known Steven for years, and immediately fell in love with him and the project. We were taking a chance on each other, sharing the same deep love and affection for the art. I was blown away by the imagery, countless stories, and timeless musical references as he took me through the tapestry of beautiful photographs and mood boards that covered his office walls. The images spoke to me, and at that very moment, I felt like Alice staring straight down the rabbit hole, about to venture into a whole underground fantasy world of beauty, magic, thrill, and excitement.

Always a risk taker, I was up for the challenge. I wanted to dig deep into my emotions to *feel* the character and project her emotions externally as I became Ali and saw things through her eyes. Meanwhile, I got cracking on some original music. I had the opportunity to cover some of my favorite soul songs from childhood, ones which I had listened to and been a fan of all my life. Stemming from a past of pain and hardship, Ali would sing these songs with raw honesty and passion, pouring her heart out with every note. As a release for growing up in a small town with dreams not quite realized, Ali was about to give the word *burlesque* a whole new meaning.

By the time Bojan Bazelli's cameras started rolling, my transformation into Ali was well under way. She would then open herself up to a world of imagination, sex, power, and greed, on the path to discovering her true evolved self.

When the curtains dropped, and all was said and done, the risky decision I'd made paid off in spades. The journey I embarked on over the course of production was truly magical. I guess burlesque without risk, just isn't burlesque. And like most great stories (films and novels), the best character journeys usually begin with the help of a mentor. For me, that mentor was my costar, Cher. Working with her was a dream come true. Looking back, I couldn't have chosen a better woman to learn the ropes from, and best of all, I made a true friend through the process.

Amy—Thank you for taking a chance on me. Clint—Thank you for your belief, endless support, and trust in me. Steven—Thank you most of all for your guidance, unbridled imagination, and for your love. It was an honor to be a part of *Burlesque*, the movie. I think we made something truly special…something Etta, Josephine, and Fosse would be proud of! And I mean that from the bottom of my heart.

—CHRISTINA AGUILERA

WELCOME TO BURLESQUE

I've always been fascinated by the organic, unstructured nature of early burlesque. Today, most people think of burlesque as a 20th-century convention rooted in second-rate striptease, when in actuality, burlesque was a comedic entertainment that became popular in Europe in the early 18th century as a form of musical and theatrical parody. It was entertainment created for the middle class and was always based in comedy. By the time it reached the height of popularity in late 19th-century England, burlesque had evolved into the premier form of musical comedy, parodying current events, popular songs, or books and adapting them to suit the medium's broad and often risqué style. It was pure, bona fide pop culture. It wasn't until burlesque gained popularity in the United States that the art reformed itself to resemble the more sexually charged performance that we know today.

I wanted to make a movie that embodied the kind of unadulterated entertainment enjoyed by audiences of the original version of burlesque. I wanted to tell a simple story, with familiar characters, set in an unusual, extraordinary, and fantastical environment. I wanted to captivate an audience, and I wanted to do it in a world populated by beautiful, funny, intelligent, and empowered women who celebrate the classic styles of feminine masquerade. I wanted to use a theatrical setting and a musical backdrop, so I could also pay homage to, and draw inspiration from, the great musicals from Hollywood's Golden Age.

I wanted to reintroduce the world to *burlesque.*

I wrote the part of Ali with Christina Aguilera in mind. I just could not imagine any other actress for the role. I will never forget the first time Christina walked into my office. She had the confidence of a lioness, with the most piercing blue eyes, perfect porcelain skin, an uncanny wisdom and intelligence, and a completely intoxicating vulnerability. I joined her on the couch, put my hand on her knee, and said, "I am not making this movie without you. "She laughed the purest, most honest and contagious laugh. It stole my heart. Christina was the first actress to sign on for *Burlesque,* and from the beginning, she never ceased to amaze everyone involved with her tireless commitment to the film and her innate acting ability. She also delivered, unsolicited, three original songs she wrote and performs in the movie, and they are spectacular. I will be eternally grateful for her collaborative spirit, and her belief and faith in me as a filmmaker.

Similarly, Cher was my first and only choice for the role of Tess. I refused to think of another actress playing the role. My friend, David Geffen, had read the script, and on his own volition, got it to Cher and told her she had to read it for the role of Tess, which really set things in motion. After months of shamelessly chasing her, Clint Culpepper, president of Screen Gems, producer Donald De Line and I finally bamboozled a meeting with Cher at her home in Los Angeles. Cher was elegant, beautiful, articulate, and hilariously funny. She was, and is, the coolest chick I have ever met. We spent hours talking and listening to her stories: *The Sonny and Cher Show, Moonstruck,* every up and down of her unremitting career. When we finally got around to talking about the film, she said, "[Tess] is me. I want to do this movie." And the next day, she turned down the role.

I couldn't take no for an answer, so I did what I do best: I wore her down. Clint and I lured her to my office to see the entire movie, storyboarded and pasted all over my walls, with photos and concept art that articulated the look, feel, and tone of the film. Cher said yes that night. Then she turned us down three more times before we started, principal photography. This was the way we'd work throughout the film. It was our way of wrestling the very best out of each other and ourselves. She did rewrites on the set; finished prerecording her musical numbers in the last nanosecond; made last-minute wardrobe decisions. She elevated the movie every single step of the way. I love her dearly and I am proud to call her my friend.

Christina and Cher were the foundation of our dream-team cast of extraordinary actors, including Stanley Tucci, Kristen Bell, Julianne Hough, Cam Gigandet, Eric Dane, Alan Cumming, and Peter Gallagher. I am infinitely grateful for the caliber of talent that I've been blessed to work with on this film.

The planning of any film is a meticulous and arduous process. But embarking on a project of the size and scope of *Burlesque* is even more daunting. In December 2008, nearly a year before shooting was to begin, our executive producer, Stacy Kolker Cramer, introduced me to choreographer Denise Faye and her partner Joey Pizzi. Denise's understanding of burlesque as an art form, to say nothing of her intelligence, experience, and passion, made her the perfect addition to the film. Denise was more than a choreographer. She worked with me to conceptualize every dance number, every set, costume, and makeup. She and Joey brilliantly conceived and staged the musical numbers.

Cinematographer Bojan Bazelli and I share a very similar aesthetic and love of film. From our first meeting,

(CONTINUED)

(CONTINUED FROM PREVIOUS)

I knew Bojan understood my vision for the movie, and I trusted that he would add his own invaluable artistry. I envisioned a dramatic, jewel-toned look for *Burlesque,* with chiaroscuro-style lighting, inspired by the candle-lit paintings of LaTour and Caravaggio's complex play of light and dark, as well as Bertolucci's *The Conformist,* Fosse's *Cabaret,* and Kubrick's *Barry Lyndon.* I wanted all of this and a timeless but modern feel. Easy, right? No. In fact, it was very difficult and challenging, but Bojan and I decided together this was our goal and he beautifully and artfully translated these varied sources into a seamless, cohesive, dramatic, and original look for the movie.

Gary Steele, our production designer, was instrumental in conceiving our main character: the burlesque lounge. We watched dozens of movies, researched thousands of photos, and explored everything from 17th and 18th century opera houses to the great deco theaters built in Los Angeles in the 1920s. After months of research, we spent huge amounts of time testing flooring, mocking up prosceniums and choosing the colors, gilding, moldings, fabrics, wallpaper, the aging and sheen for the walls, mirrors, lampshades, and sconces—all of the elements that tell the story of the club. Gary paid staggering attention to even the smallest detail. Amazingly, Gary's very first rendering of the burlesque lounge is almost exactly what you'll see in the movie.

Michael Kaplan completed the vision of the film with the most stunning, dynamic, and show-stopping costume design any director could ever hope for. Aside from being Clint's best friend, Michael is hands down one of the best in the business. His research left no stone unturned, his design was inspired, his craftsmanship was impeccable, and his dedicated team were the utmost professionals. The result is undeniable—a sumptuous feast that elevates every character, song, and dance.

Decades of polished experience can be found on our crew list, and I cannot say enough how incredibly grateful and blessed I am to have worked with such talented individuals—Scott Strauss, Buck Damon, Ginny Katz, Peggy Eisenhauer, Dana Belcastro, Dave Goldberg, and Geoff Hansen, just to add a few more names to the aforementioned. I would like to extend a special "I love you" and thank-you Amy Pascal, for believing in *Burlesque,* for your insightful guidance, generous soul, for your love of film and musicals, and for giving me the opportunity of a lifetime by greenlighting this movie. I would like to thank my good friend Donald De Line for coming on as a producer and giving the movie instant credibility. Last but not least, thank you Clint Culpepper for convincing me to write *Burlesque,* then convincing the entire industry of its worth, for your contagious vision of *Burlesque,* for teaching me how to make a movie, and for your fearless, unwavering dedication to this film.

—*STEVEN ANTIN, WRITER/DIRECTOR*

I wanted to maintain a certain simplicity for Ali's makeup, one that would be honest to the life of a girl growing up in Iowa, but making it obvious that she is a girl who has done her homework, dreaming of the "big time" while paging through fashion magazines. I used soft mauves on her lips and a very blushed coral on her cheeks. Even when Ali gets dressed up to impress, the same palette is just intensified, keeping all the same shades.
— Kristofer Buckle,
Makeup Artist to Christina Aguilera

THERE WAS A LOT OF DISCUSSION AROUND THE OPENING SCENE
OF THE FILM. IT'S A GREAT EXAMPLE OF THE INTERCUTTING
NARRATIVES OF SONG AND STORY THAT APPEARS THROUGHOUT.
WHEN ALI'S STILL IN IOWA, SHE'S SINGING KARAOKE IN AN
EMPTY BAR, BUT IN A MANIPULATION OF TIME AND SPACE,
YOU'RE ALSO SEEING THE GIRLS SINGING BACKUP FOR HER IN
THE BURLESQUE LOUNGE IN LOS ANGELES. ONE'S DURING THE
DAY; ONE'S AT NIGHT. THE IMAGES AND THE WORLDS ARE SO
DIFFERENT FROM ONE ANOTHER. IT'S ALMOST A FORECAST OF
WHAT SHE'S HEADING INTO AND ONLY REALLY MAKES SENSE
WHEN YOU REALIZE YOU WERE SEEING TESS'S BURLESQUE
LOUNGE. BUT DURING THE OPENING SCENE, WE WANTED TO
JUXTAPOSE THE TWO DISPARATE WORLDS, WITHOUT SHOWING
TOO MUCH OF EITHER. WE THOUGHT THE BEST WAY TO DO IT, TO
MAKE THE BURLESQUE LOUNGE LOOK REALLY DIFFERENT FROM
IOWA, WAS BY FOCUSING ON THE LIGHTS. WE HAD ROWS AND
ROWS OF FOOTLIGHTS THAT WE PUT EVERYWHERE. SO EVERY
TIME WE SHOWED THE GIRLS, WE HAD LIGHTS BEHIND THEM,
WHICH SIGNALED A GLITZY, NIGHTCLUB LIFE. IT WAS
A SIMPLE WAY OF FURTHERING THE STORY.
— STEVEN ANTIN

I GREW UP HERE, AND I'VE OFTEN BEEN AROUND
HOLLYWOOD AND VINE AT A CERTAIN TIME OF
THE DAY, AT A CERTAIN TIME OF THE YEAR.
AND THE SUN SETS ALMOST RIGHT IN THE
CENTER OF HOLLYWOOD BOULEVARD
AND CREATES THIS INCREDIBLE LIGHT THAT
BLASTS THE STREET. IT REFLECTS OFF THE
SLICK TERRAZZO HOLLYWOOD WALK
OF FAME SIDEWALKS.
— STEVEN ANTIN

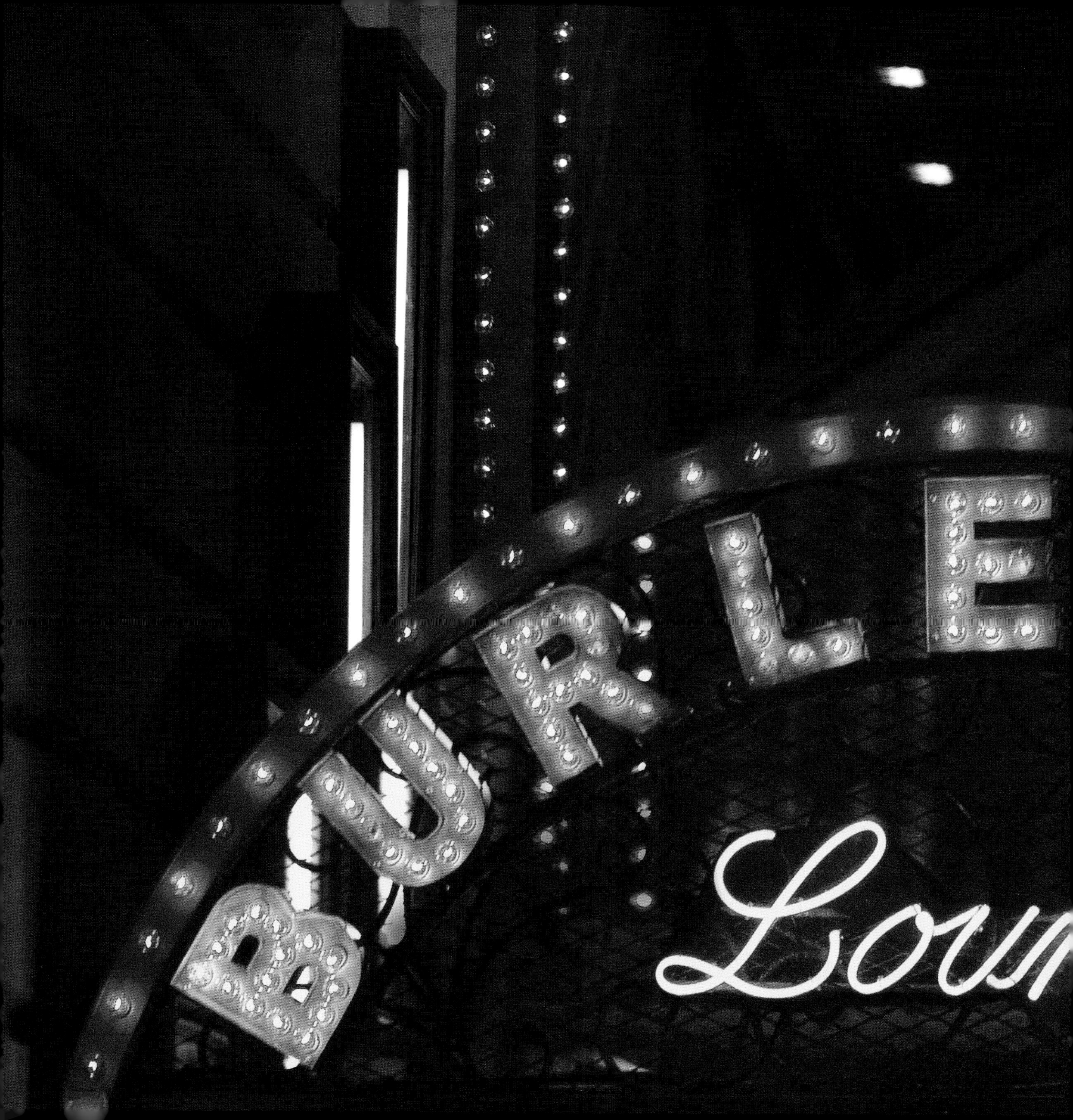
BURLE
Lou

*BURLESQUE IS ABOUT DANCING AND
SINGING AND COMEDY AND FUN.
IT'S SOMETIMES RISQUÉ, AND ALL
THE TIME SEXY, BUT NEVER SEXUAL.
IT'S EVERYTHING BURLESQUE
WAS AND EVERYTHING IT WAS
MEANT TO BE.*
— STEVEN ANTIN

Cher's longtime collaborator, Bob Mackie, designed her costume for "Welcome to Burlesque." It's an important point in the film, as it's the first time Ali, and the audience, meet Tess. The original song sets the tone for the film, and Bob's design immediately lets us know who Tess is and what we're in store for. As you can see, the final costume looks just like Bob's sketch!
— Steven Antin

I DIDN'T WANT THE AUDIENCE TO SEE
ANYTHING THAT WASN'T THROUGH ALI'S EYES,
SO THE FIRST TIME WE SEE THE BURLESQUE
LOUNGE, THE WHOLE BURLESQUE LOUNGE, IT'S
FROM ALI'S PERSPECTIVE. IT JUST FELT LIKE
THE RIGHT WAY TO TELL THE STORY.
— STEVEN ANTIN

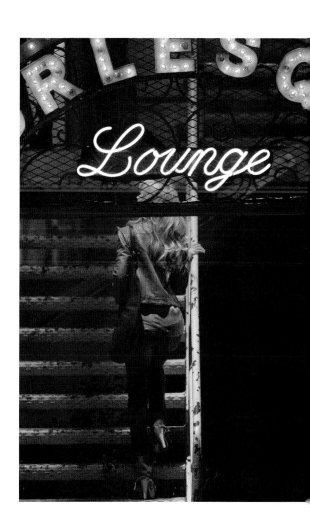

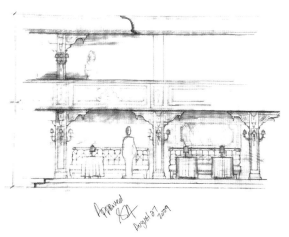

Jon Gary Steele had a bigger vision for the lounge than I did, and I'm glad we went in his direction. I had imagined something more intimate, with a proscenium and 1920s feel to it. I thought the thrust would be about fifteen feet, with black flooring and chandeliers and lights, and the lounge would have different textures all over the place. But Gary was constantly pulling pictures and images from French bistros and restaurants and opera houses. He looked at everything he possibly could and pieced it all together. Everything was so detailed, even the wood on the floor was specially chosen. The mirrors were a real process. We aged them for weeks and weeks until we came up with what we thought was the right aged, emulsified look, then we added layers of wax to create layers. We did the same thing to the walls, adding layers of paint and gloss, so even though everything's brand new, it looks like it's really old. When you walk into the lounge, you walk into another world.
— Steven Antin

The design of the burlesque theater was the most challenging, crazy, and fun part of working on the film. We wanted it to reflect Steven's wish to have it look like it was straight out of 1920s or 1930s Los Angeles, and yet, have the audience feel like once they came inside from modern Los Angles, they felt like they stepped into 1930s Paris or Berlin.

The art department spent weeks researching the period to pull different ideas together to form our thoughts on the look and feel of the space. We looked at opera houses and theaters from all over Europe, but the more we saw Parisian restaurants and brasseries, and the way they used mirrors and gilded moldings, we knew that was the direction we wanted to go in. Steven wanted the entire theater to have the look of faded elegance, so everything—from the booths and tables to the drapes, wall sconces, and mirrors—was built and then aged and distressed to give it a worn-in look.

In order for the cameras to capture uninterrupted action from the theater, bar, and backstage, the different rooms of the theater were built and connected to each other on a two story set at the studio. Since the actual set was being built, painted, dressed, and lighted by Peggy, Bojan, and the others, we had to build Denise and Joey rough duplicate mock-ups of the different set pieces so they could rehearse and work out the numbers properly.

The entire art department had so many talented people, including art director Chris Cornwell, set decorator Dena Roth, assistant art directors Charlie Campbell and Al Lewis, lead man John Naehrlich, art deptartment coordinator Candice Muriedas, construction coordinator David Elliott, and head scenic Artist David "Goldy" Goldstein. I couldn't be more proud of the work they and their teams have done.
— Jon Gary Steele, Production Designer

I never got used to putting on
"guy-liner." It was kind of a big
production every time I had to do it.
But it does make my eyes pop!
— Cam Gigandet

The pivoting and gamboling mirrors behind the bar
were Gary's idea. So was the zinc bar top. I was dubious
about it, but he showed me pictures of Hollywood bars
from the 1920s, which we thought would be the time the
lounge would have been built, and there they were.
It was a challenge to make all of the musical numbers
look different when the stage didn't have many moving
parts. We used the bar as an alternative dance space to
stage the number for the girls and Alan, and used
the mirrors to reflect the stage.
— Steven Antin

ALI WALKING INTO THE LOUNGE
FOR THE FIRST TIME IS A BIT LIKE
ALICE FALLING DOWN THE RABBIT
HOLE. YOU REALLY FEEL THAT, AS SHE
DESCENDS THE STAIRCASE AND THE
FIRST PERSON SHE SEES LOOKS LIKE
THE MAD HATTER!
— STEVEN ANTIN

Stanley brings a levity to scenes
that you wouldn't necessarily expect.
He brings a poeticism, too. There's
just so many layers to what he does
that it makes his scenes feel real and
beautiful and organic.
— Steven Antin

When I heard the words "Cher and Stanley, we're ready for you?" I never thought those words would ever come out of somebody's mouth.
— Stanley Tucci

If you like Cher, you'll love this movie.
This movie is Cher Christmas. I bet
the rates of coming-out are going to
skyrocket as a result of this film.
— Alan Cumming

Nobody knows how to be Cher better
than Cher. There's a level of excellence
that she brings to everything, and when
she walks into a room, the standards
are brought up to a different level.
You've got to step up your game with
Cher. Tess has given her life to this
craft. It's a long-faded art form, except
for this little oasis that she keeps alive.
It's a part of her, and she's a part of it.
— Steven Antin

No detail was spared. I don't know if the audience will see it, but I'm even wearing bottom eyelashes! From our nail polish to the tattoos, nothing was overlooked and nothing is boring.
— Julianne Hough

JULIANNE WAS FUN TO DRESS.
WE COMPARED HER TO
ANN-MARGRET. SHE LOOKS
GREAT AS A REDHEAD, HAD
INCREDIBLE BLUE EYES, AND
IS AN AMAZING DANCER.
— MICHAEL KAPLAN,
COSTUME DESIGNER

IN THE DRESSING ROOMS, WE USED
GLASS SO YOU COULD BE PUTTING
MAKEUP ON IN ONE ROOM AND THE
CAMERAMEN COULD BE SHOOTING
OVER THE ACTORS AND SEEING
DROPS AND BEADED CURTAINS
AND CHANDELIERS GOING UP AND
DOWN IN ANOTHER ROOM IN THE
BACKGROUND. WE WANTED TO OPEN
IT UP SO IT'S NOT JUST A ROOM—
WE WANTED TO SEE THE INNER
WORKINGS OF A THEATER.
— JON GARY STEELE

We had to color Julianne's eyebrows red, and use a lot of complementary colors for her red hair, versus Christina's blond and Kristen's brown. She has the most beautiful crystal-blue eyes, so we used colors that really bring out the blue.
— Cindy Williams,
Department Head, Makeup

Every girl has a different look in this film. They all have different personalities, and we thought they should also have different hair colors and hair styles. Kristen's wearing a brunette wig. It's a lovely ebony, Elizabeth Taylor–like, dark dark brown. She looks amazing in that color. Julianne is wearing a flaming red one. Just to die for. Very Rita Hayworth. They look great together, and since their characters play off one another in the movie, especially in the "Diamonds" number, we achieved a sort of "Gentlemen Prefer Blondes" look. But we didn't want anyone to know they were wigs, of course. The hairlines of the wigs are made of an extraordinarily fine lace that gets slightly heavier toward the cap. Every inch is pinned down tight over the girls' heads, like a second skin. Their real hair is wrapped so tightly it's flat, but we wanted to make sure that even though the wigs fit like a glove, and wouldn't move, they were still comfortable for them. This was hard during the dance numbers, which are so physical. The girls are so vibrant, whipping their hair all over the place, going upside down, really working it. The wigs had to be put on so they: one, wouldn't look like wigs, and two, wouldn't come flying off. Every minute of every take we were watching, making sure everything's still firmly attached.
— Martin Samuel, Department Head, Hair

WE HAD A WHOLE WALL OF MUSICAL NUMBERS
AND IDEAS. DENISE AND JOEY REFERENCED
EVERYTHING YOU COULD POSSIBLY IMAGINE
FROM THE LAST SEVERAL HUNDRED YEARS
OF DANCE: BURLESQUE, VAUDEVILLE, OPERA,
BALLET—EVERYTHING.
— STEVEN ANTIN

I WAS FAMILIAR WITH JAZZ, BALLET, LATIN, AND OF COURSE BALLROOM, BUT THIS FILM HAS BEEN FUN BECAUSE I GOT TO GO IN A COMPLETELY DIFFERENT DIRECTION.
— JULIANNE HOUGH

I LOVED THE IDEA OF THE BARTENDERS
WEARING BOWLER HATS AND GIVING THEM
A NOSTALGIC, EUROPEAN FEEL. WE ALL
THOUGHT THE VESTS, SUSPENDERS, AND
MORNING-STRIPE PANTS WERE REALLY COOL
LOOKING, AND WE ADDED A BIT OF MACHISMO
BY PUTTING THEM IN LACE-UP BOOTS AND
WATCH CHAINS, WHICH ADDED A VISUAL
INTEREST WHEN THEY WERE DANCING.
— MICHAEL KAPLAN

THE BAND MEMBERS DIDN'T HAVE ANY
TATTOOS, SO WE HAD A GROUP OF ARTISTS
PUTTING BIG FULL-ARM TATTOOS ON THEM
EVERY DAY. WE HAD STENCILS MADE FOR EACH
OF THE BAND MEMBERS, AND WOULD ORDER
EXTRAS IN CASE THERE WAS A MISTAKE OR FOR
A DOUBLE. FOR EXAMPLE, CAM HAS HIS OWN
TATTOO, SO WE TOOK PICTURES AND HAD AN
ARTIST MAKE A COPY. THEN WE HAD COPIES OF
THAT MADE AND APPLIED IT TO HIS DOUBLE
SO THEY LOOK EXACTLY THE SAME.
— CINDY WILLIAMS

WE USUALLY HAD THREE
CAMERAS, BUT WHEN WE
WENT TO FOUR OR FIVE,
WE'RE TALKING ABOUT THE
BIGGER NUMBERS. FOR THE
FINAL NUMBER, WE HAD A
FIFTH CAMERA DEVOTED
EXCLUSIVELY TO SUPER
WIDE-ANGLE SHOTS. WE
WANTED THE FINAL NUMBER
TO BE THE BIGGEST ONE OF
ALL, AND WE WERE ABLE TO
EXPAND THE SIZE OF THE SET
BY USING THE WIDE-ANGLE
LENSES THAT WEREN'T USED
IN THE MOVIE BEFORE THEN.
— BOJAN BAZELLI,
DIRECTOR OF PHOTOGRAPHY

As a choreographer, my first step is to figure out how each musical performance will tell the story while supporting, and visually expressing, the characters' journeys. We weave and meld together the plot and characters' development through music and dance. In order to create these meaningful moments, we spent months referring to the script pages directly preceding number, just to see precisely what the character had just lived through. Then, we'd meditate on what type of a number might best serve the script. What type of song? What type of dance? As a result, the numbers organically grew out of the characters' actions and desires. The story informed our choices, but the characters were the driving forces. This process continued into the rehearsal studio with my co-choreographer and longtime friend Joey Pizzi, and then on until the very last day of the shoot. *Burlesque* was an enormous undertaking. Joey and I wanted to create a magical and captivating world, and Steven encouraged us and the choreography team, all with unique talents and specialties, to explore new directions and mix classic and new styles of dance and movement.
— Denise Faye, Choreographer

You have dancers on tables, dancers on the stage, dancers on the bar, behind my head, doing some pretty wild things. I was afraid to look back!
— Cam Gigandet

"DIAMONDS" IS A FABULOUS NUMBER. I'M
ALL WRAPPED UP AND SLIDE DOWN THE
METAL BEADED CURTAIN. IT TOOK ABOUT FIVE
MINUTES TO GET WRAPPED BECAUSE I DON'T
HAVE ANYTHING HOLDING ME UP! THE BAD
THING WAS THAT AFTER A FEW TAKES THE
CURTAINS LEFT A LOT OF MARKS. IT LOOKED
LIKE I HAD RUG BURN ALL OVER MY BODY! IT
TOOK ABOUT THREE WEEKS FOR THEM TO GO
AWAY, BUT THE PAIN FEELS GOOD WHEN YOU
KNOW IT'S GOING TO PAY OFF!
— JULIANNE HOUGH

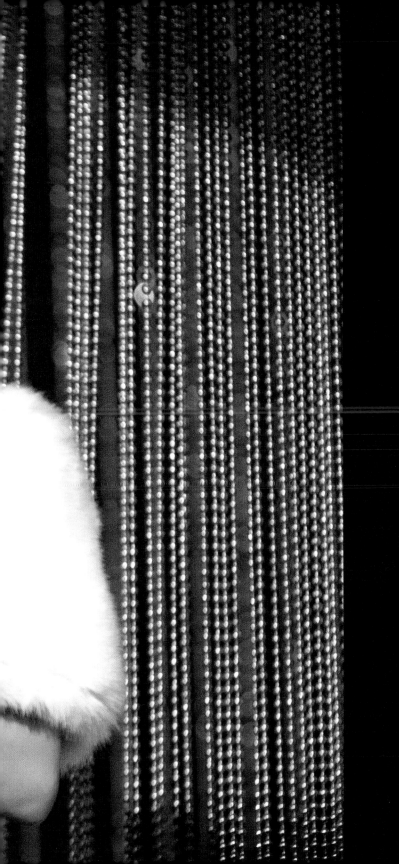

WE USED A CURTAIN MADE OF
SWAROVSKI CRYSTALS. ACTUALLY,
SWAROVSKI CRYSTALS WERE
INCORPORATED INTO MANY OF THE
COSTUMES, TOO. THEY HAVE A VERY
SPECIFIC LOOK AND REFLECTIVE QUALITY
TO THEM. THEY'RE IN THESE INCREDIBLE
COLORS, AND THEY CERTAINLY DON'T
LOOK CHEAP! THEY'RE PAINSTAKINGLY
EVERYWHERE IN THE FILM.
— STEVEN ANTIN

I've always been cast as the sweet or goofy girl, but Nikki is quite a handful. I thought it would be a great challenge to play a sort of entitled woman, but keep her slightly lighthearted and a little funny so the audience doesn't downright hate her. It's good to play bad. There are fewer rules and you can do what you want.
— Kristen Bell

THESE TATTOOS ARE NOT MINE. THEY'RE FOR THE CHARACTER, BUT I WISH THEY WERE MINE. I FEEL VERY COOL WHEN I PASS THE MIRROR!
— KRISTEN BELL

These costumes are fantastic. There are a lot of beads and sometimes you're sewn into your costume. And oftentimes you can't take it off. Nikki's costumes needed to be a little more fabulous than everyone else's, because Nikki always tries to be more fabulous. If someone's wearing pink, Nikki wants to be wearing hot pink. And her coat is this huge shag rug thing— it's completely over the top. And that's exactly what Nikki is.
— Kristen Bell

It looks like Kristen's not wearing anything, but between the catsuit and the mesh, she's completely covered.
— Steven Antin

73

We knew we had to try to make the scene fun and funny to take advantage of Kristen's great comedic skills. It was Denise and Joey's idea to create the dental chair that spins around and goes up and down, and Kristen's timing and instincts elevated the number to something greater than we imagined.
— Steven Antin

KRISTEN HAS SUCH A
DIFFERENT LOOK IN THIS
MOVIE. TO COMPLEMENT
THE DARK HAIR, WE ADDED
TATTOOS AND TOUGHER,
SHARPER MAKEUP.
— STEVEN ANTIN

MARCUS ISN'T A BAD GUY;
HE'S JUST THE WRONG GUY.
— ERIC DANE

PETER DID HIS HOMEWORK ON
THE CHARACTER. HE INVENTED
AN ENTIRE BACKSTORY THAT
BROUGHT THE CHARACTER TO
LIFE. AND ERIC COULD HAVE
PLAYED THE CHARACTER AS A
MOUSTACHE-TWIRLING VILLAIN,
BUT THE CHOICES HE MADE LET THE
AUDIENCE BELIEVE THAT MARCUS
WAS MORE THAN THAT.
— STEVEN ANTIN

We had to find ways to make
every number look different.
We were always looking for ways
the light could surprise you.
— Jules Fisher,
Theatrical Lighting
Designer

It's hard to put a price on any of these costumes. They're so labor intensive, and they go through many different hands. And when you see the dancers wearing the costumes, what you can't see is the work that went into them. For example, the chain dresses aren't interchangeable. The fabric understructures of the costumes, including their fishnet hose, were individually dyed to match the girls' skin tones to make them look nude. So it gives the illusion of nudity, but also gives us something to anchor the chain onto. It was incredibly time consuming. Different fabrics and bras dye differently, so you can't put them all into one vat. Everything had to be dyed on its own, and individually matched to its corresponding pieces. The costume-makers themselves were more like special-effects people. Working with metal is completely different from working with fabric. Besides actually connecting all of the chains, we had to meld them to the individual girls' bodies. Each one is a perfect fit. When dancers move, their muscles expand, and the costumes had to move with them. The costumers painted clear rubber washers gold to allow the structure to stretch. This allowed the costumes to give a little when the dancers moved. So much of what they did was invisible to the eye.
— Michael Kaplan

Most lighting in motion pictures is very static. The electricians and gaffers and cinematographers come in the morning and they work for hours to set up the lighting. Then you shoot all day long and never change it, whereas in a musical, light cues happen with the music, in between the beats of the music, and follow emotional lines. We use stand-ins on the set to establish light cues, sometimes for days in advance of shooting. This way, when a dance number has twenty cues, they're all already set.
— Jules Fisher

WE WANTED EVERYTHING TO BE BEAUTY, BEAUTY,
BEAUTY, SO EVERY IMAGE IN EVERY SHOT IS LAYERED.
A LOT OF PEOPLE DO THAT IN POST-PRODUCTION,
BUT WE CHOSE TO DO IT IN-CAMERA. IT'S OLD-SCHOOL
FILMMAKING THAT TAKES A GREAT DEAL OF TIME. AND
THEN THERE'S THE CHOREOGRAPHY! YOU NEED MANY
CAMERA MOVES AND DIFFERENT ANGLES TO GET IT
ALL. AND LIGHTING A BIG ROOM IS ANOTHER THING.
WE'RE CREATING LAYERS, WITH THE PARTICLES OF
SMOKE PICKING UP THE INDIVIDUAL SHAFTS OF LIGHT.
AND THEN WE'RE DOING THINGS THAT PROBABLY
NOBODY ELSE WILL NOTICE, BUT WE THOUGHT THEY
WERE IMPORTANT, LIKE CREATING SHADOWS AND
IMAGES ON THE WALLS, AND BOUNCING THE LIGHTS
OFF OF MIRRORS OR THE REFLECTIVE FLOOR.
THIS WAS MORE COMPLICATED THAN FILMING
A SIMPLE ROMANTIC COMEDY, WHERE YOU DO
RELATIVELY STANDARD LIGHTING AND CAMERAWORK
AND HOORAY! BUT FOR THIS GENRE? FOR A MUSICAL?
IT'S A COMMITMENT!
— STEVEN ANTIN

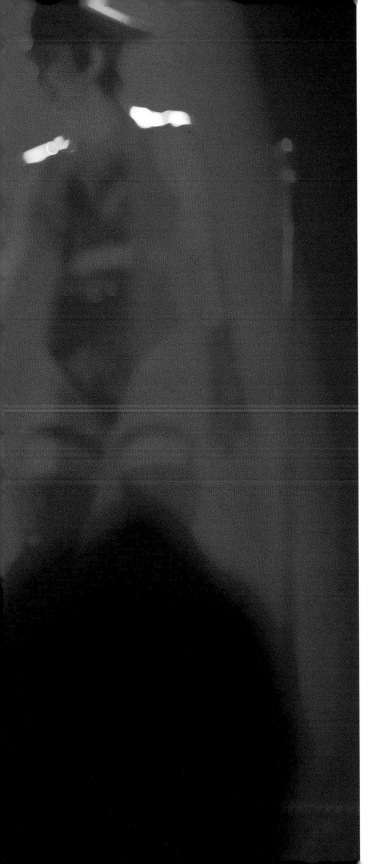

I DID STRONG, LONG EYES
WITH A SEVERE CHEEKBONE AND
MAGENTA LIPS TO GIVE
A TOUGH "FETISH" FEELING,
BUT KEPT THE UPPER LID
ALMOST BARE SO THAT WE
WOULDN'T LOSE HER EYES
UNDER THE SHADOW OF THE
BRIM OF HER HAT. I ORIGINALLY
DESIGNED THIS LOOK WITH
A BURGUNDY GLITTER LIP, BUT
STEVE THOUGHT IT MIGHT
BE TOO MUCH FOR THIS
IMPORTANT SCENE.
— KRISTOFER BUCKLE

When I think of burlesque, I think of the color red. The color really makes a statement throughout the film. We added lots of reds, lots of tones, throughout the entire musical, especially during the numbers when there is a significant amount of red.
— Bojan Bazelli

We invented a story about who
would have been doing the
lighting of the club and tried
to get into his imaginary head.
We wanted to communicate a
live theatrical experience in
the film so the audience felt
like a concertgoer or a club
patron. Our goal was to make the
performances believable.
— Peggy Eisenhauer
Theatrical Lighting Designer

I always do homework before starting a new lighting project, but I was particularly interested in the lighting for this film because I actually worked on a summer stock burlesque show when I was sixteen. It was one of the last touring burlesque-style productions. One of the biggest challenges was how period-specific should we be. We researched what the lighting would have been for a show at the height of burlesque, what a space like this would have used, what would have been held over decades after. And then how far over the top we could go with it.
— Peggy Eisenhauer

We needed to get outside the lounge to open things up. We did a bunch of shots that were not second unit or just beautiful shots with Ali and Jack on the motorcycle.
— Steven Antin

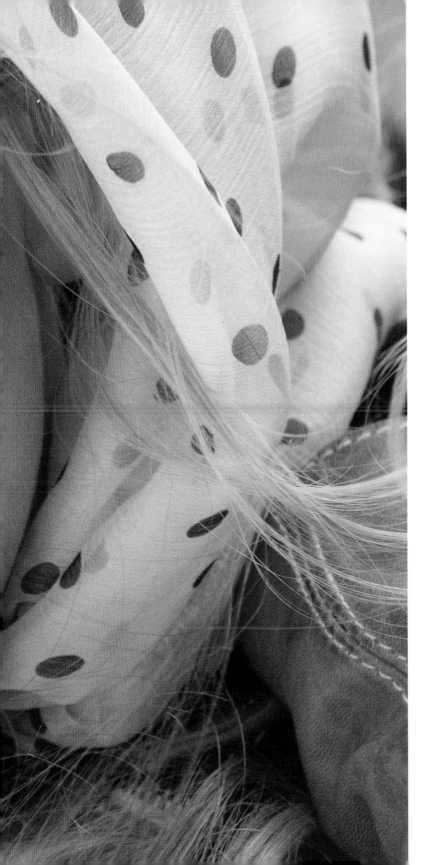

Creating Ali's many looks for the film was a fun and collaborative process. Luckily, Steven's a man who understands beauty and appreciates glamour, so I felt free to push the envelope. Due to the ambitious scheduling of the musical numbers, Steven and I would often have impromptu meetings about makeup. After exchanging ideas on set or over lunch, I'd go off and sketch. One time, he wasn't sure how the ball eyelashes I had created for "A Guy Who Takes His Time" would translate from paper to real life, so he came to Christina's trailer where she ran through the number for him. He loved them!
— Kristofer Buckle

NOT THAT HOLLYWOOD ISN'T A
VIBRANT PLACE, BUT WE TRIED TO
KEEP IT A LITTLE MONOCHROMATIC
SO ANY TIME WE ENTER THE CLUB,
THE CONTRASTS ARE STRONGER AND
THE COLORS MORE VIBRANT.
— BOJAN BAZELLI

The costumes needed to exist in the
atmosphere of the burlesque lounge.
They needed to look and feel as if they were
the work of Tess and Sean, and not those of
a Hollywood costume designer or remnants
snatched up from a Las Vegas revue.
— Michael Kaplan

During "Something's Got a Hold on Me,"
the girls had big curly hair and we did really
big lashes and tried to make them look like
china dolls with big full lips and bright pink
all around the eyes and cheeks.
— Cindy Williams

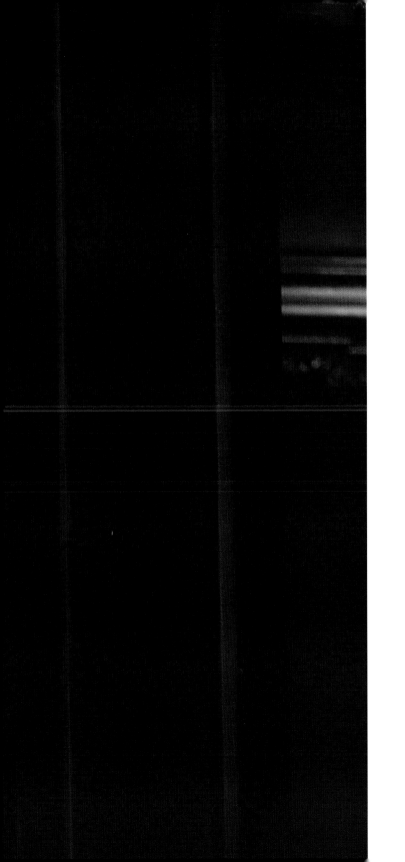

CHRISTIAN LOUBOUTIN DESIGNED
A ONE-OF-A-KIND PAIR OF SHOES
SPECIFICALLY FOR CHRISTINA TO WEAR
IN THE MOVIE. THEY'RE SPECTACULAR,
AND SERVE AS AN IMPORTANT STORY
POINT FOR HER CHARACTER.
—STEVEN ANTIN

I WANTED TO KEEP THIS
LOOK THEATRICAL, FUN,
AND FEMININE. I USED A
TRADITIONAL BALLERINA
EYE AS INSPIRATION, BUT
USED A PALE PINK GLITTER
ON THE LID AND SPIKY
LOWER LASHES SO THE
LIGHT WOULD ANIMATE
THE MAKEUP.
— KRISTOFER BUCKLE

THE STAGE WAS ABOUT
THIRTY DEGREES HOTTER
THAN THE REST OF THE
ROOM BECAUSE OF ALL
THE LIGHTS. IT WAS
EXCRUCIATING FOR THE
GIRLS UP THERE.
— STEVEN ANTIN

When planning a film, you can't shoot all the musical numbers back-to-back. They're a tremendous amount of work for the dancers and it would cause injuries. Plus, you'd wind up killing some of them.
— Steven Antin

I PRESENTED THREE OR FOUR
SKETCHES TO CHRISTINA FOR
THIS NUMBER AND SHE WENT
RIGHT FOR THE ONE WITH THE
HANDS. ACTUALLY, THE HANDS
ON THE BUM ARE MINE!
I STOOD THERE IN THE FITTING
ROOM WITH THE DRESS DUMMY
AND THE HEAD SEAMSTRESS,
RUTH, TRACED AROUND
MY HANDS CUPPING THE
MANNEQUIN'S BACKSIDE.
— MICHAEL KAPLAN

THIS NUMBER RELIED ON IMAGES
FROM WEIMAR GERMANY.
DARK EYES BUT LONGER ALMOND
SHAPES AND WITH METALLIC
PEWTER INSTEAD OF BLUE.
UPPER AND LOWER HEAVY LASHES
WITH A RED LIP AND A BLACK
SWAROVSKI CRYSTAL AS
A BEAUTY MARK.
— KRISTOFER BUCKLE

S. Martin Shot List "EXPRESS"
Express Shot List
A & B Cameras

ⓐ → SIDE VIEW CRAWLING THROUGH ARMS MIR
→ HANDS PICKING UP MAKE-UP THIN
→ CLOSE UP OPENING MOMENTS
→ CLOSE-UP SNAPS
→ CLOSE-UP ANKLE ROLLS
→ SIDE VIEW OF BUTTS
ⓑ → EVERYthing REVERSE THROUGH MIL
→ CLOSE ON SLAPS (GROUND / CHAIR
ⓑ → CLOSE HAND THRU LEGS
→ IN MIDDLE & ABOVE — BIG DANC
→ Highlight CHAIR SPIN
ⓐ → GET EACH GIRL SINGLE (ish)

131

CHRISTINA IS A WOMAN WHO
LOVES TO WEAR MAKEUP, AND SHE
LOVES TO DRESS UP AND HAVE
DIFFERENT HAIRDOS.
SHE'S A THROWBACK TO THE
GOLDEN AGE OF HOLLYWOOD.
— STEVEN ANTIN

I HAD A VERY SPECIFIC THING I WANTED TO DO AT THE
END OF THE NUMBER. I WANTED CHRISTINA'S LIGHTING
TO FADE AND THEN COME UP BEHIND HER AS SHE RAISED
HER ARMS AND CAST DRAMATIC SHADOWS. ACHIEVING
THAT ISN'T DIFFICULT, BECAUSE IF YOU PUT A VERY
STRONG LIGHT BEHIND SOMEONE THEY'LL CAST A SHADOW,
BUT GETTING IT TO LOOK RIGHT ON FILM, GETTING THE
SHADOWS TO READ CORRECTLY, IS ANOTHER THING. IT WAS
ALL A MATTER OF DEGREES. WE DECIDED TO PUT A CERTAIN
COLOR LIGHT BEHIND A SHEER BLUE CURTAIN, WHICH
WOULD LOOK RIGHT AGAINST THE GREEN DRESS.
IT'S A PAINFULLY BEAUTIFUL NUMBER, AND IT WAS
PAINFULLY DIFFICULT TO SHOOT. WE WANTED A JEAN
HARLOW-ESQUE KIND OF SATINY SLIP FOR CHRISTINA'S
SOLO. WE WRESTLED WITH HOW TO BEST CAPTURE THE
VISUAL IMPACT OF THE COMBINATION OF A BLONDE
WOMAN WITH VIBRANT RED LIPS IN AN ACID GREEN COLOR
AGAINST A PALE BLUE BACKDROP FOR ALMOST THREE DAYS.
THE COLOR COMBINATION COULD BE EITHER INCREDIBLY
BEAUTIFUL OR TOTALLY SICKENING.
— STEVEN ANTIN

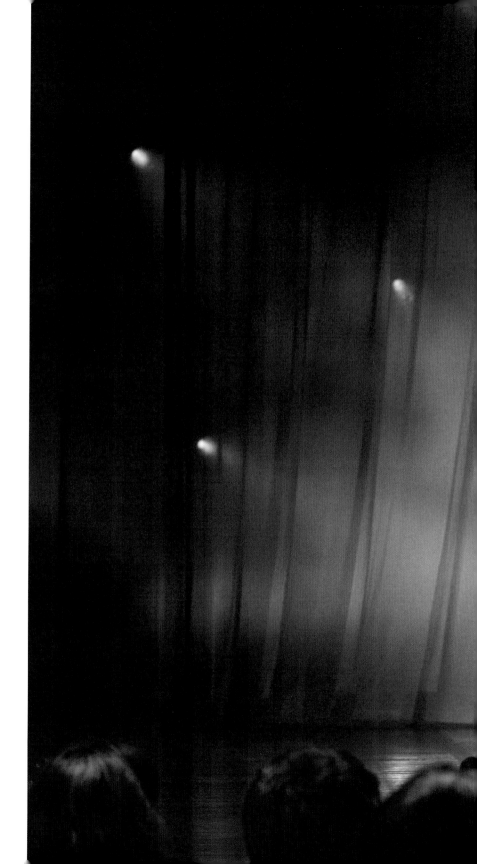

This ballad needed to have a simple formality. Liquid eyeliner with a wispy lash, glowing skin, and ruby lips were the perfect balance to the green satin gown; and kept Ali looking vulnerable.
— Kristofer Buckle

— Scrap Idea —
Do Classic Tight Liner
soft lash — featheresh
skin — and red lip.

Bound to you

139

What you hear in the film is the
actual Frank Sinatra arrangement of
"That's Life" from 1966. When I was in the
recording booth, there were a couple of
bits I wasn't getting quite right.
The sound engineer asked if I would like
to hear how Mr. Sinatra did it. I totally
copied Frank Sinatra. Isn't that exciting?
Afterward, I thought, gosh, what did
I do today? Well, I danced on top of a
bar, singing to the track Frank Sinatra
recorded in a big, fun movie. I think that
was my defining moment.
— Alan Cumming

I think if you really want to be an artist, you want to tell a story. And how better to tell it than with your whole body? Victoria and Shannon aren't just artists interpreting a dance, they were also people putting their legs in places you were worried about.
— Alan Cumming

My favorite things are these spats.
I'm hoping to steal them after.
— Alan Cumming

Julianne and Alan had met about ten minutes before shooting the wedding scene. He didn't recognize her as a brunette, and asked if, during their dance, she could manage a twirl. She laughed and said she could handle it.
— Steven Antin

WE KNEW WE WANTED TO DO SOMETHING
GRAND FOR THE FINALE, BUT WHEN STEVEN
WANTED LETTERS—EIGHT FOOT LETTERS—
ON THE STAGE WE KNEW WE HAD OUR WORK
CUT OUT FOR US. ART DIRECTOR CHRIS
CORNWELL AND ASSISTANT ART DIRECTOR
CHARLIE CAMPBELL SOMEHOW GOT THOSE
BIG LETTERS TO WORK, AND LOOK GREAT,
ON THE STAGE.
— GARY STEELE

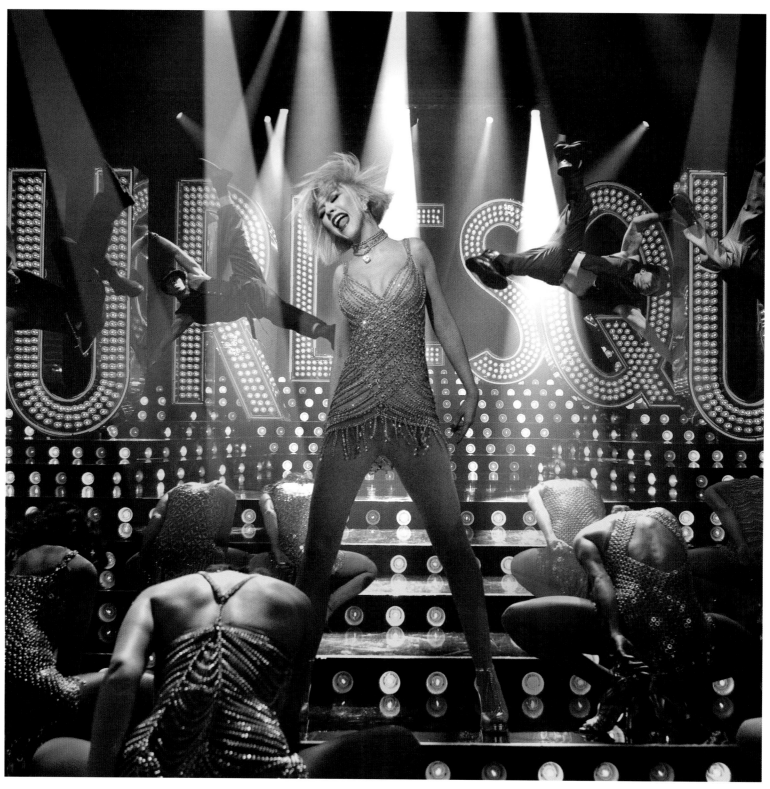

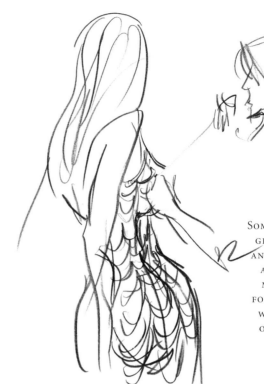

SOMETIMES A CERTAIN LOOK LOOKS
GREAT ON ONE GIRL BUT NOT ON
ANOTHER. WE HAD TO SOMETIMES
ALTER THE LOOKS A LITTLE TO
MAKE THEM COMPLEMENTARY
FOR EACH GIRL. SO EVEN THOUGH
WE MIGHT BE DOING THE SAME
OVERALL LOOK FOR A NUMBER,
EACH ONE HAD VARIATIONS
WITHIN IT.
— CINDY WILLIAMS

TONE DOWN ORANGE & YELLOW

LOSE THE CRYSTALS

INNER SOFTER & BROWN

FINALE

I THOUGHT USING GOLD AND ORANGE
SHADOW WOULD COMPLEMENT
THE GOLD CHAIN COSTUME. I KEPT
THE SHAPES "FELINE" TO GO WITH
THE INTENSE, SEXY MUSIC AND
CHOREOGRAPHY. A RED LIP ADDED
A HIT OF COLOR TO KEEP IT FROM
LOOKING MONOCHROMATIC.
— KRISTOFER BUCKLE

BURLESQUE

CHER
CHRISTINA AGUILERA
ERIC DANE
CAM GIGANDET
JULIANNE HOUGH
ALAN CUMMING
PETER GALLAGHER
with KRISTEN BELL
and STANLEY TUCCI

Written & Directed by STEVEN ANTIN
Produced by DONALD DE LINE

Executive Producers
DANA BELCASTRO
STACY KOLKER CRAMER
RISA SHAPIRO

Director of Photography BOJAN BAZELLI, ASC
Production Designer JON GARY STEELE
Edited by VIRGINIA KATZ, A.C.E.
Music Supervisor BUCK DAMON
Executive Music Producer CHRISTINA AGUILERA
Executive Music Consultant CHRISTOPHER "TRICKY" STEWART
Choreography by DENISE FAYE *and* JOEY PIZZI
Costume Designer MICHAEL KAPLAN

SCREEN GEMS PRESENTS
A DE LINE PICTURES PRODUCTION

First published in the United States of America in 2010 by Universe Publishing,
A Division of Rizzoli International Publications, Inc.
300 Park Avenue South
New York, NY 10010
www.rizzoliusa.com

Art Direction and Design by Townhouse: Anton Aparin and Nick Vogelson

Costume sketch on page 24 courtesy of Bob Mackie.
Red curtain photograph and black and white photographs on pages
50, 87, 115, 126, 134, 167, and 168 by Willa Mamet.
All other photographs by Stephen Vaughan.
Illustrations on back of jacket, flaps, and pages 13, 49, 108, 109, 113, 128, 160, 161, 164,
165, and 167 by and © Andrea Selby a.k.a. Luma Rouge.

2010 2011 2012 2013 / 10 9 8 7 6 5 4 3 2 1
Printed in the USA
ISBN-13: 978-0-7893-2201-2
Library of Congress Catalog Control Number: 2010929006

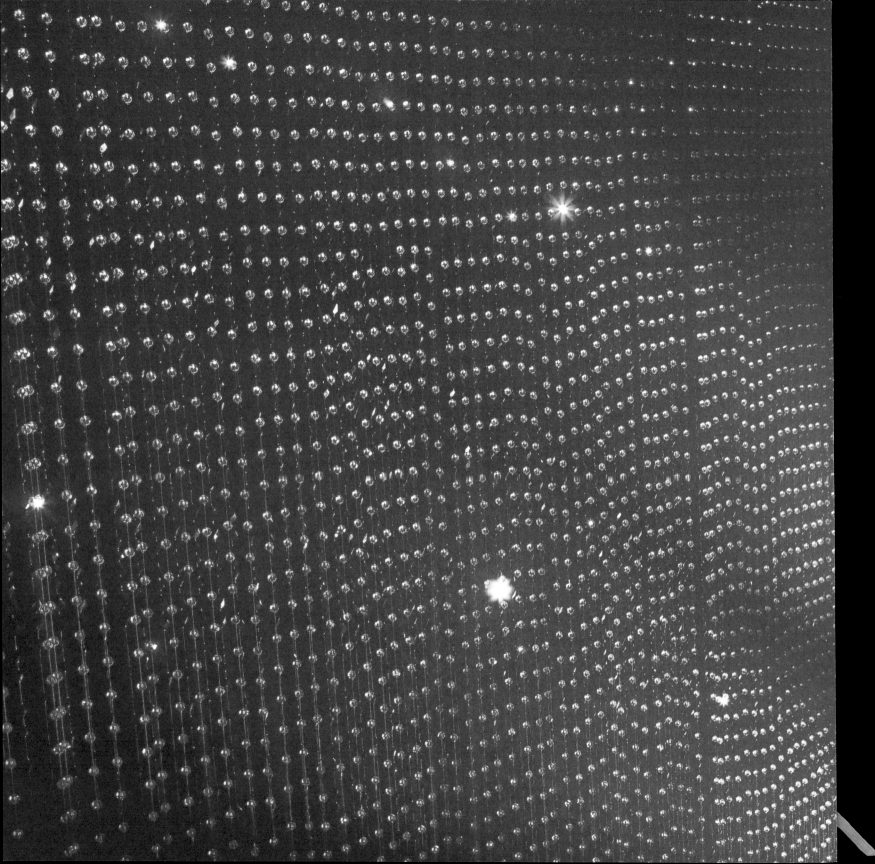